D1497803

Development of Regional Airports

WITPRESS

WIT Press publishes leading books in Science and Technology.
Visit our website for the current list of titles.
www.witpress.com

WITeLibrary

Home of the Transactions of the Wessex Institute, the WIT electronic-library
provides the international scientific community with immediate and permanent
access to individual papers presented at WIT conferences. Visit the WIT eLibrary
at http://library.witpress.com

Development of Regional Airports

Theoretical Analyses and Case Studies

Edited by:

M.N. Postorino

University of Reggio Calabria, Italy

WITPRESS Southampton, Boston

Editor: M.N. Postorino
University of Reggio Calabria, Italy

Published by

WIT Press
Ashurst Lodge, Ashurst, Southampton, SO40 7AA, UK
Tel: 44 (0) 238 029 3223; Fax: 44 (0) 238 029 2853
E-Mail: witpress@witpress.com
http://www.witpress.com

For USA, Canada and Mexico

WIT Press
25 Bridge Street, Billerica, MA 01821, USA
Tel: 978 667 5841; Fax: 978 667 7582
E-Mail: infousa@witpress.com
http://www.witpress.com

British Library Cataloguing-in-Publication Data
A Catalogue record for this book is available
from the British Library

ISBN: 978-1-84564-143-6

Library of Congress Catalog Card Number: 2009926709

*The texts of the papers in this volume were set
individually by the authors or under their supervision.*

Contents

Introduction
Regional airports development: background

The importance of the air transport system is widely recognized not only as a mean to quickly cover long distances, but also as an economic engine for all communities. Aeronautical industries, airports and airlines are some of the main actors that, each one in its own field, compete for the air transport market.

The capability to cover long distances in reduced time with respect to other means of transport is one of the most successful factors that have contributed to the growth of the air transport system; as an example, the technological developments and the increase of civilian routes between Europe and North America have caused the end of intercontinental travels by ships, that at the beginning of the 21st century represented the only means of transport to go from the old to the new continent.

The continuous development and the results obtained by the aeronautical industries have increased the level of safety, the comfort and the efficiency of the system.

Today, the air transport system provides the only means that can be used to reach remote or inaccessible areas, or regions not well served by land transport systems; it is irreplaceable for medical emergencies and humanitarian assistance; it is a source of integration between different communities as well as a source of economic development for the region served by air carriers.

In short, the air transport system plays not only an important role as means of transport but also as a social connector and economic engine.

The main actors of the air system are airport planners, air companies (mainly grouped in full carriers vs. low-cost companies) and users (passengers and/or freights) that can produce important demand levels at airports, thanks to their travel choices.

In the air transport system, airports are the nodes of the system, while routes are the links among nodes. In many countries, and especially in European countries, location and characteristics of the airports are defined at central level, while links are established thanks to the services offered by the air carriers.

Airports are important elements of the air transport system because they represent interchange nodes among land transport systems and the air transport system, and also because they are the air traffic control centres. The main characteristics of an airport depend on the expected number of passengers and movements, the performed function and the kind of routes being offered.

In terms of passengers and movements, airports can be defined as:

- primary, if the number of yearly passengers is greater than five million per year;
- regional, otherwise.

The EU also classifies airports as:

- community airports, if the number of passengers is greater than ten million per year;
- national, if the number of passengers ranges from five to ten million per year;
- large regional, if the number of passengers ranges from one to five million per year;
- small regional, if the number of passengers is less than one million per year.

Furthermore, according to ANNEX 14 (ICAO), an airport can be classified depending on the airport traffic density as:

- light: if the number of movements during the peak hour is less than 15 for each runway, or if for all the runways it is less than 20;
- medium: if the number of movements during the peak hour ranges from 16 to 25 for each runway, or if for all the runways it ranges from 20 to 35;
- heavy: if the number of movements during the peak hour is greater than 26 for each runway, or if for all the runways it is greater than 35.

Depending on the performed function, an airport can be classified as:

- hub
- feeder.

A hub is an interchange node for an air carrier that offers a hub-and-spoke service. Particularly, flights coming from multiple origins converge into the airport (hub) from which new flights start toward multiple destinations (spokes). The hub-and-spoke structure has been used to increase the number of served destinations (in fact, starting from a generic origin one can reach whichever destination going through the hub) and to obtain greater load factors for each aircraft (in fact, point-to-point services to guarantee the same number of destinations from each origin could not have a satisfactory level of demand from the point of view of economic convenience). In this way, the production costs can be reduced while the quality of offered services can be increased.

Then a hub airport is not necessarily a primary airport (following the previous definition), but an airport where an air carrier has established the hub of its hub-and-spoke service.

The choice of an air carrier to locate its own hub at a given airport depends on different factors as:

- key position with respect to the potential users;
- location near a big city or a metropolitan area able to generate high volumes of traffic flows other than those in transit;

- airport high capacity and efficient management in terms of take-off and landing systems, in order to reduce delays and congestion effects;
- passenger terminals able to guarantee an efficient transfer from an aircraft to another one.

The management of the airport is crucial for the success of a hub-and-spoke system; in fact, when airports are not able to support and manage the more and more increasing volume of traffic, users experience negative effects as delays, flight cancellation and baggage loss.

A feeder can be defined as an airport supporting the hub or in other words as the spoke of a hub-and-spoke system; however, flights can also be guaranteed by other companies, thanks to the alliances and code-sharing networks. Nowadays, feeder services at many airports classified as 'regional' are flanked by point-to-point services often offered by low-cost companies both toward national and international destinations.

Inside the hub vs. feeder airport classification, another distinction can be made between mega-hubs (as in Europe, London-Heathrow, Paris Charles de Gaulle, Frankfurt am Main), with a large catchment area that makes them attractive also for point-to-point trips but are too expensive for many low-cost companies; and secondary hubs (as in Europe, Barcelona, Copenhagen, Lisbon, Manchester, Rome, Vienna, and so on) which operate as both feeder airports for mega-hubs and smaller hubs for certain regions.

Finally, depending on the kind of routes being offered, airports can be classified as:

- first level airports: intercontinental and international links covering distances greater than 3,000 km; airports supporting this kind of routes are equipped to work with high traffic levels and are generally hubs for many companies;
- second level airports: international links covering distances less than 2,000–3,000 km;
- third level airports: national and international links covering distances in the range of 500–700 km.

A particular characteristic of the air system is its continuous development both in terms of aircraft technology (larger and faster aircrafts, greater flight autonomy also for smaller aircrafts, lower fuel consumption, large use of computer and automatic systems to guarantee both the efficiency and the safety during the flight, and so on) and service organization (hub-and-spoke rather than point-to-point service, air company alliances, frequent flyer programs, business models, and so on).

Among these factors, low-cost companies and regional jets (a kind of aircraft used for medium-short distances, characterised by high cruise speed as regards to the aircraft class, low pollution level and reduced landing/take-off distances) have characterized the air transport system in the last years.

They have as a common aspect the potential re-evaluation of regional (third level) airports. In fact, low-cost carriers prefer to use regional airports providing point-to-point links rather than hub-and-spoke services, changing thus the tendency of the last decades. Similarly, regional jets can be considered the preferential kind of aircraft for regional airports, because they are characterized by low capacity in terms of offered seats per aircraft (and therefore they are competitive as loading factors in low-level demand areas) and by reduced distances required for landing/take-off operations; low-level demand and short runways are common factors of regional airports.

The main differences among low-cost carriers and full service (or traditional or flag) carriers are the following:

- low-cost carriers do not use Computer Reservation Systems (CRS) as selling channel, but they prefer internet or phone calls;
- check-in, handling and maintenance are generally outsourced services;
- on-board services (as meals, magazines, and so on) have been reduced or eliminated (for this reason low-cost companies are also called 'no-frills');
- fleet is generally formed by the same kind of aircraft (most low-cost companies use Boeing 737 aircraft);
- the offered routes are generally medium-short and point-to-point inside a continent (e.g., EU or USA);
- low-cost companies are independent air carriers, i.e. any network/code sharing among companies;
- they often operate at regional airports where airport fees are low, capacity is generally high and there are attractive slots; then, air companies can reduce operational costs, avoid delays and maintain short turn-round times.

A general consequence of the low-cost business model used by the different air carries has been the reduction of the air fare and the re-evaluation of some less classical destination areas, which have thus improved their attraction as tourist destinations. Furthermore, in most cases they have helped the development of regional airports as well as the development of the nearest territory and the reduction of congestion at some hubs due to the different distribution of the traffic volumes.

The considerable increase of the air transport demand, mainly inside Europe and the USA, but also nowadays in some Eastern countries as China and India – where more low-cost companies started successfully their services – produces congestion problems both along the routes and above all at the main airports.

In fact, it is well known that mega-hubs and hubs gather the most part of the traffic volumes while the remaining airports have a lot of residual capacity that can also be used to reduce hub congestion. Congestion is a significant, negative consequence of the hub-and-spoke structure because it produces an increase of the overall trip time (both for users and air companies); higher probability of baggage loss; delayed or cancelled flights; and higher values of pollution due to the aircraft and land vehicle movements, as well as to the induced land traffic to and from the airport.

On the other hand, the development of regional airports can have as a consequence not only a reduction of congestion at the main hubs but also the socio-economic development of the areas close to the airport.

In this context, and in order to re-evaluate the role of regional airports, the understanding of both the demand characteristics from/to regional airports and the techniques of the air transport supply simulation is a fundamental step to verify the effectiveness and efficacy of the system structure as regards to the different involved actors (air companies, users, and society).

The overall framework taking into account the different aspects of the air transport system simulation is depicted in Figure 1.

Air transport demand depends on air services that in turn are offered at a given airport depending on the number of passengers, i.e. the demand level at the airport.

There is an evident feedback between the future level of air services and the passenger airport choice. The airlines will provide air services at airports only if there is a financial convenience; this means a sufficient number of passengers choosing that airport in order to make feasible a given level of air services. Similarly, the number of passengers choosing a given airport depends on the air service level at that airport. The explicit simulation of this interaction is important to verify the airport development potential (within a larger airport system) and then which are the more suitable policies to support such development.

When demand at an airport and offered services are mutually consistent, the system reaches an equilibrium that can then be evaluated in order to obtain the system performances as regards airport managers, passengers, airlines and society.

The simulation of the demand–supply interactions and then the demand distribution among the various available airports should take into account the (limited) capacity of the system (Figure 2) and the possible constraints that can exist and contain the capacity (prescriptive or physical constraints, urban areas in the neighbourhood, and so on).

A first case is when the predicted demand/supply values and the corresponding traffic flows (in terms of passengers, and thus aircraft movements) do not satisfy the current airport capacity. If the airport capacity can be increased (consistently with possible external constraints as urban areas in the neighbourhood, noise constraints, available space to physically extend the airside, and so on) a new situation can be simulated and evaluated by taking into account the monetary costs required to increase the capacity.

A second case is when the predicted demand/supply values and the corresponding traffic flows do not satisfy the current airport capacity as before, but the airport capacity cannot be increased as required because the necessary interventions are inconsistent with the external constraints. In this case, the realization of a new airport can be considered and the evaluation should take into account the overall airport system in terms of demand, supply and interactions between airports.

Because the passenger's airport choice depends on the air services at that airport and because the airlines services are linked to the profitability of their services, modifications of the cost structure, the available services and the operational rules can modify the passengers' choices to use a given airport and the choices of airlines to provide a given service.

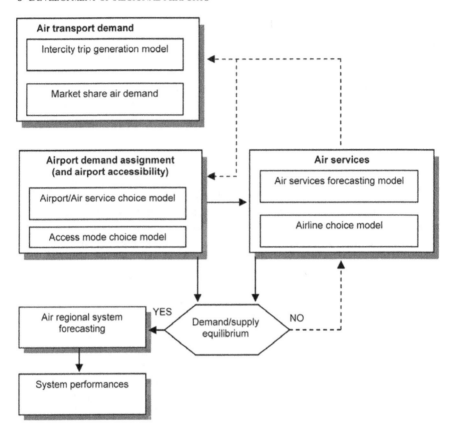

Figure 1: Layout of the air transport system simulation.

Then, a suitable model should be able to simulate how a given set of policies can influence, on the whole, traffic levels at each airport. This means, to an increasing level of detail, the simulation of the future scenarios in terms of economic activities and land use, as well as the development of land transport systems and the consequences in terms of traffic distribution. Particularly, high-speed trains are expected to be competitive with the air transport services for medium-distance trips and they should be taken into account because of the effects they produce on the overall traffic levels at a given airport. For example, high-speed train services between a medium-size city, also served by a regional airport, and a main urban area served by a hub airport will have a great influence on the air traffic level at the regional airport, both in terms of direct trips and transfer trips, especially if the high-speed train also serves the hub airport at the main urban area. In fact, passengers can use railway instead of air services for city-to-city trips (direct trips), but also to reach the hub and then choose the best airlines to complete the travel (transfer trip). The regional model should take into account this kind of effects and interactions between competitive modes both in terms of predicted demand levels and airport distribution in a given region.

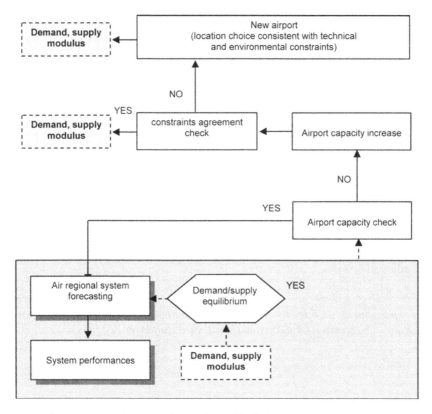

Figure 2: Capacity constraints and possible limits to airport development.

The above description, also depicted by Figures 1 and 2, provides a theoretical modelling background; actually, many problems can arise when the different parts have to be modelled; for example, air service at airports is an airline decision; the hypothesis of boundary condition stability to simulate future developments can be unrealistic in some contexts; modelling of the airport user choice process as well as relationships between air supply and demand to simulate equilibrium is a really complex task; and so on.

Following the previous considerations, the main goal of this book is to provide a summary of the key aspects related to the simulation and analysis of the potential development of regional airports.

In order to give an outline of the main tendencies and policies in many countries, the EU (Chapter 1) and Asian (Chapter 2) situations are described. Then, after an overview concerning the main economic aspects linked to the development of regional airports (Chapter 3), several approaches used in the literature to simulate the air demand at airports are described, with an application to a regional airport in South Italy (Chapter 4). Air demand at airports is the result of a choice process involving also the choice of airlines operating at the airport itself and the choice of the access mode, depending on the airport accessibility characteristics:

these aspects are discussed in Chapter 5, together with a case study conducted in Greater London. An operational methodology, developed and applied in the Netherlands to simulate the air demand–supply equilibrium at airports, is described in Chapter 6, thus facing practical and theoretical aspects. Finally, the crucial role that can be played by low-cost carriers is explored for the Australian regional airports (Chapter 7), by considering key factors as air fares and number of competitors on each route.

Acknowledgements

I wish to thank Kenneth Button, Yu-Chun Chang, David Hensher, Stephane Hess, Eric Kroes, as well as Andrew Collins and Zheng Li for their invaluable contribution and for having supported with great availability this editorial project. Furthermore, I would like to thank Carlos Brebbia who believed in this book and gave me the opportunity to realize it, as well as his editorial staff, particularly Elizabeth Cherry and Brian Privett, for their help in many stages of the editorial process.

Maria Nadia Postorino
Department of Computer Science, Mathematics, Electronics and Transports,
University 'Mediterranea' of Reggio Calabria, Reggio Calabria, Italy

1

Economic aspects of regional airport development

K. Button
George Mason University, USA

Abstract

Transport has important effects on the nature of local economies and on their overall development. The focus here is on the particular role that air transport, and in particular airports, can play in the regional economies. Public policy has always been interested in ensuring that adequate and appropriate air transport infrastructure is available to serve regions, be it for strict economic reasons or for social and political purposes. Where to invest, the form of investments and its scale have long been within the remit of economic analysts, and more recently the matters of finance and air service retention has attracted mounting interest. The role that economics can play in better understanding many of these issues is considered here.

Keywords: airports; airlines; economic growth theory; market instability; low-cost airlines.

1 Introduction

Transport has always played an important role in economic development. It is no accident that the dominant cities of antiquity grew on major trade routes, often on seaports or on rivers that were the major carriers of inland trade. Railway stations served a similar role in the 19th century and more recently good road access has been seen as important. Airports have also played a major role in many parts of the world in allowing economies, sometimes national, and also at a regional level, realize more of their economic potential.

Air transport is a relative new mode but has grown rapidly. It is particularly important for long- and medium-distance movements of people and high-value/low-volume commodities. It serves a particular purpose where for economic or geographical reasons it is not viable to construct the fixed track infrastructure needed for road or rail transport. In many cases, it is seen as essential to ensure social and political cohesion in large countries, or those with terrain not suited to surface modes. It is a very flexible mode of transport not strongly tied to a network of inflexible tracks or infrastructure,[1] and, although the larger ones can be expensive, airports are relatively cheap to build and operate compared to an extensive rail or road system. The tendency to name airports after local dignitaries also makes them attractive for politicians.

But there are some downsides too, one of which is the difficulty of retaining air services; we pay particular attention to this later. They are often monopolies and this can lead to the exercise of market power by their owners combined with laxity in management – X-inefficiency. State-owned facilities, where rent seeking is not usually the norm, are particularly prone to the latter.[2] Air transport is also noisy and airports can involve considerable land-take and surface access challenges. Consequently, rather than just focus on the potential economic benefits for a region of having air transport access, issues of economic institutions are considered, and the ways they may facilitate the provision of airport infrastructure and its optimal use.

2 Transport and economic development

Airports are seldom, if ever, a strict catalyst for local economic development. An area is only likely to enjoy substantial and sustained economic growth if it has inherent potential. Airports are also not free-standing entities; they require complementary surface infrastructure even if developed at appropriate locations. Economists are not good at understanding why economic growth takes place, the types of industry that drive it at any particular time, or the way that it is distributed geographically. If they did then the planned economies that were created in the post-Second World War era would be thriving. Consequently picking 'winning' investments in regional airports is challenging.

Traditional neo-economic (exogenous) growth theory focused on factor endowments as the driver of growth. A region would grow if it had a suitable mix of economic factors that could be exploited. If it did not have the factors that was needed then there was the possibility of importing them – labour being the most obvious, but also some raw materials. In free market conditions, labour would move to the regions where it was needed, attracted by the high wages there that reflect scarcity rents. Capital and raw materials would, in turn, move to regions with excess labour attracted by the returns offered from combining with labour. In the long run everything would balance out and all regions would grow at the same pace. Overall in this environment, aggregate growth could only occur as more factors became available (e.g. a higher birth rate or human survival rate, or because of technical progress which was seen as a random event). Policies aimed at maximizing the mobility of factors of production were about all that governments could advance.

The intellectual works initially of Kaldor [2], but more recently of Lucas [3] and Romer [4, 5], coupled with the empirical analysis of Barro and Sala-i-

Martin [6, 7], on economic convergence, have brought into question whether region's economies do converge, and, even if they do, whether the rate of convergence is significant. This is the 'new growth theory'. The argument moved to whether growth was, in part, endogenous within regions leading to divergences in economic performance – the richer getting richer at the expense of the poorer who were entrapped in a downward spiral of poverty. Basically, richer regions attracted only the most highly skilled and energetic workers from the poorer regions, whilst capital was retained because of factors such as economies of scale (Kaldor's argument), or because the knowledge base of these regions stimulated technical progress (Lucas's and Romer's argument) which attract investors' interests.[3]

In terms of transport, the traditional view was that appropriate transport was needed to allow for migration to take place, and countries used to provide subsidized passage for immigrants. The new growth theory treats it somewhat differently; it is seen as a possible way for less developed areas to become more attractive to investors and as a mechanism to bring in skilled labour. This does not mean that investment in an airport, or expansion of an existing one, will, *per se*, lead to local economic development, but it can allow the region to more fully exploit its potential.

3   The economic impacts of airports

Airports do not just appear in markets, they are planned and their operations are carefully regulated by local, national and often, in the case of major hubs, international bodies. There are positive and negative external economic effects, combined with numerous non-economic influences that determine whether an airport is built, its scale and its operational design. They also have features that give them advantages in combining with airlines to provide transport in specific circumstances, and for the carriage of particular types of traffic. Geography, for example can be particularly important in determining the number of airports required and their type. Table 1 [9] shows the number of airports that European countries have by size. It is noticeable that geographically large countries with sparse populations and difficult surface terrain tend to have numerous small airports and few large ones, for example Finland and Norway.

At the macro-level, there have been intensive debates about the role of infrastructure in enhancing the economic productivity of a country or a region, and this has influenced policy choices. Early aggregate econometric work in the 1980s [10] indicated a correlation between infrastructure, mainly transport investments and productivity growth at the national level, but subsequent analysis at more disaggregate regional, urban and project level showed much less impact [11].

There are few explicit studies that have sought to undertake a full regional economic impact assessment of an airport [12, 13]. The task is not an easy one. Measuring local economic impacts of airport investment is challenging and studies have often over-estimated them. The main problem is to assess the opportunity costs involved in the airport investment. Even if the traffic forecasts and resources needed are corrected forecast, the inputs that are entailed have a cost elsewhere in the economy and, unless all markets are perfect, this can be underestimated in a partial equilibrium impact analysis. There are also issues of counterfactuals; what would have happened to the regional economy if new airport infrastructure had not been provided [14]?

Table 1: Commercial airports in selected European countries (2004).

Country	Passengers				Total airports
	Less than 100,000	100,000–1 million	1–5 million	More than 5 million	
Austria	0	4	1	1	6
Denmark	7	3	1	1	12
Finland	10	10	0	1	21
France	37	20	8	3	68
Germany	18	10	14	6	48
Greece	16	15	6	1	38
Iceland	10	3	0	0	13
Ireland	9	2	1	1	13
Italy	11	4	9	2	36
Norway	25	13	5	1	51
Spain	4	16	10	6	36
Sweden	21	20	2	1	44

The local implications of investing in airport infrastructure can be divided into four types, each with different temporal horizons.

- *Primary effects.* These are the short-term benefits to a region from the construction of an airport – the design of the facility, the building of the runways, the construction of the terminals and hangars, the installation of air traffic navigation systems and so on – and the resultant income and employment multipliers associated with this.
- *Secondary effects.* These are local economic benefits of running and operating the airport – employment in maintaining the facility, in handling the aircraft and passengers, in transporting people and cargo to and from the terminal and so on. These secondary effects can be extremely important for some local economies in terms of employment, income and, for local government, taxation revenue.
- *Tertiary effects.* These stem from the stimulus to a local economy resulting from firms and individuals having air transport services at their disposal. These differ for those living in hub cities, compared to those on a spoke or having no major carrier. Hubs offer more direct flights favoured by business travellers. But the hub also benefits those on the spokes because without a hub-and-spoke structure many would find it difficult to travel long distances at all. Hubs allow interconnectivity. In the United States, over half of the 15,000 city pairs served by a major carrier have less than one passenger per day.

- *Perpetuity effects.*[4] These reflect the fact that economic growth, once started in a region, becomes self-sustaining and may accelerate. An airport can change the entire economic structure of a region – it can shift its production function. This type of dynamic economic impact of an airport is the most abstract and the most difficult to quantify. It has been little researched but examples can be seen in the transformation of small agricultural island economies into tourist destinations and the growth of high-technology regions around major airports such as Dulles, Washington and Logan, Boston in the United States.

Getting a good handle on the magnitude of these effects is not easy, and relies on three broad methodologies: questioning local businesses and stakeholders, economic multipliers and input–output analysis, and econometric modelling. All have their weaknesses. For example, econometric analysis requires prior specification of the causal relationships while input–output analysis tends to be static in its orientation and is heavily data reliant. Additionally, most analysis tends to focus on the first three categories of impact (primary, secondary and pecuniary), and neglect any estimation of a perpetuity effect. In part, this is because most impact studies are linked to planning horizons that are relatively short term. Despite all the caveats, there is ample evidence that airports in the appropriate place can stimulate high-technology development[5] and tie regions into the international economy [16].

4 Factor movements

While regional airport analysis has generally been concerned with making more and better use of local resources, transport also plays an important role in moving productive resources between regions. The classic economic assumption of factor endowments is less applicable in the 21st century.

Traditionally, the most mobile factor of production has been capital, and this mobility has grown as transport has developed. Raw materials have also been moved to allow their combination at places of manufacture. Even in primitive times, stone was often moved long distances by water for the construction of religious and ceremonial buildings. Mass migrations of people also occurred, often as the result of conquest or as people have sought to find food or jobs.

More recently, air transport has been instrumental in allowing new forms of migration as well as the continuation of some more traditional forms. This has involved, for example movements of large numbers of highly skilled workers to places of demand. The movement of Indian computer engineers and the like to meet demands in the United States during the 1990s is an example. While there has always been a tradition of skilled and specialized workers migrating to find work – the mediaeval cathedrals of Europe were the result of such mobility – the speed, extent and duration of modern migrations is of a different scale and form. Temporary migration is now more common as labour can easily and relatively cheaply return to home after a period of time. This was not possible before the advent of the steam ship and railways, but even then it was expensive and time consuming. Air transport has changed this.

The importance of air transport, and regional airports, in facilitating labour mobility has been little explored [16]. Where it has been examined, it has tended to look at larger airports and permanent migration. This is a major issue, it is the large airports that tend to be the gateways for mass migration over long distances, and it is these airports that handle most legal issues associated with migration.[6] The gradual institutional freeing up of labour markets within the European Union, together with the availability of 'cheap' labour from many of the former transition economies (the former Soviet satellite states), has provided an opportunity for medium distance, short-term migration [17].

The growth of the service sector, the emergence of more flexible manufacturing techniques, the reduction in trade-barriers and the creation of more sophisticated financial markets has led to greater mobility in production and in capital movement. In particular, labour markets have become more malleable and workers more mobile. This has been explored to some extent in general terms – for example since the admission of Poland to the European Union in 2004 some 465,000 Polish workers have joined the United Kingdom labour market[7] – but mainly from the perspective of its economic implications for national and regional GDP or in terms of the social problems that may arise. There has been little done recently, however, looking at the role of transport innovations and migration.[8]

Air transport facilitates easier migration of workers, makes it possible for short-term migration and allows migrants to maintain contact with their home country. Within larger countries, such as the United States, there has also been a growth in long-distance 'week-day' migration as spouses working in different parts of the country reunited at weekends and work apart during the week. As Abella [18] has pointed out, 'International migration of skilled persons has assumed increased importance in recent years reflecting the impact of globalization, revival of growth in the world economy and the explosive growth in the information and communications technology.'

Our interest here is to look at how the new air transport environment has affected two particular features of the labour market: first, complete (or at least long term) migration of workers and second, and to a smaller degree, extra long-distance commuting behaviour.[9] The emphasis is on the primary effects of air transport in facilitating migration. It is not concerned with the secondary effects of air transport in terms of the relocation of businesses or stimulating particular industries, such as tourism, that may subsequently lead to changes in levels of labour migration, or in the role of air transport in leading to retirees and others simply moving home.[10]

Labour migration takes place for a multiplicity of reasons and changes in air transport markets are unlikely to have a large aggregate effect. Where there may be important impacts are in particular sectors of the labour market or in particular geographical corridors. This has often coursed debates about the implications of migration on the local economy, not least in places such as the United Kingdom where the influx of migrants been sudden and unexpected. There is also a growing interest amongst economists in the wider role of transport in factor mobility for designing policy responses to conditions where endogenous growth seems to dominate.

Air transport seems to be in many cases a facilitator of these changes. Labour migration, in its scale and in its changing composition, including greater emphasis on circulation and temporary migration, has in many cases been shaped by changes in the availability, frequency and costs of air travel. It makes the initial migration itself more viable and, by facilitating cheap return trips, reduces the longer term social costs of being away from kith and kin even when the migrant locates considerable distances from traditional gateways.[11]

The reforms in air transport regulation have overcome many of the previous limitations of air transport as a significant form of mass mobility; costs were a significant barrier to air travel as were the frequency and convenience attributes. Low-cost airlines, and their knock-on effects on the legacy carriers, have changed this. As a result they have impacted on labour markets in several ways, but mainly through reducing travel costs and increasing accessibility. Effectively, they reduce the transaction costs of international labour migration and, all else being equal, by shifting the balance between the costs and returns of migration have contributed to the increase in factor mobility.

For individuals, the cost of being away from home is high (mental and physical stress, the cost of separation, etc.), for others the cost of travelling may be more important. For all, air transport lowers total migration costs. Some can visit relatives more often. Others can at least afford getting to their destination. There is also the induced demand for migration that is made possible by lower air transport costs. Agricultural Mexican workers could not, for example, move to Canada to work temporarily if it were not for air transport because obtaining transit visits to travel via the United States can prove very difficulty for low-income individuals.

There seems to be a change in attitudes towards flying as low-cost services have grown. Low-fare services available from a local airport seem to be changing consumers' perceptions about flying generally and consequently are having an effect on travel patterns. In many cases, as with Ryanair in Europe that serves numerous small airports with radial structures of routes, it is not simply about vacations and visiting a second home but also seems to stimulate people to apply for jobs abroad and may facilitate working far from home. Wizz Air, the Hungarian air carrier, is a leader among several low-cost airlines transporting planeloads of Poles, Hungarians and others to Western Europe with one-way fares starting at less than €20 (about $26), including taxes [20]. Nearly one million East Europeans have moved to the United Kingdom, Ireland, Sweden, Germany and other member countries after the European Union expanded from 15 to 25 nations in 2004.

In particular, there has been increased air traffic between several of the new European Union member countries with significant migrant flows into the United Kingdom on routes where there have been expansions of low-cost carrier activity; not only Wizz but also Centralwings (a subsidiary of Lot Polish Airlines), the Slovenian carrier SkyEurope Airways and others. Just taking

Poland as an example of service growth, in 2000 there were 5 scheduled services between Poland and the United Kingdom; by 2006 this had grown to 27 scheduled services linking 12 Polish cities and 12 United Kingdom airports [21].

While the causality between changes in the airline market and labour migration patterns is not all unidirectional, workers are increasingly participating in labour markets far from home and airlines have responded by creating an informal new travel category alongside the traditional business, leisure, and 'visiting friends and relatives' traffic breakdown. Airlines often call this 'ethnic traffic' to reflect the cultural diversity of these travellers. Many carriers have even adapted their business models to cater for these ethnic travellers because of the relative reliability and predictability pattern of their demands that offset the relatively cheap fares paid. Ethnic travellers are for instance highly regarded by low-cost airlines like Wizz and SkyEurope Airways.

While official statistics do not capture this particular sub-class of traveller, one can glean some indication of the growth in this ethnic traffic, at least in Europe, by looking at the conventional visiting friends and relatives (VFR); most of the growth in VFR being in migrants making visits to their homeland. Table 2 takes the two primarily low-cost United Kingdom airports, Stansted and Luton, and compares the number of inbound passengers for 2000 and 2005. As can be seen, VFR traffic grew by 198% over the period to become the largest single component of inbound traffic. At the national level, a similar picture emerges with VFR traffic growing from less than 2.5% of European Union passengers in 1997 (when there were 15 member countries to about 15% by 2005; albeit with 25 members).

Table 2:   Inbound passengers from the European Union to the United Kingdom using Stansted and Luton airports.

Passenger type	Passengers 2000 (million)	Passengers 2005 (million)	2000– 2005 change (%)	Percentage of total in 2000 (%)	Percentage of total in 2005 (%)
Business	0.9	1.8	98	22	17
Leisure	1.6	4.0	150	39	38
Visiting friends and relatives	1.6	4.8	198	39	45

There have been significant changes in demographic patterns over the past 40 years that affect the context in which residential/work place decisions are made. Portes [22] suggested the existence of transnational communities – a community that spans borders – boast their key assets, shared information, trust and contacts. This has led to a more flexible economic structure that often involves longer distances between home and work and between spouses for part of the time. This type of behaviour is not migration in the traditional sense, but involves an extended, regular commute, and often, spending parts of the week away from home.[12]

While explicit data on the extent of long-distance commuting involving air travel is small,[13] some indication of its importance can be seen indirectly in the high grow rate of extended-stay hotels in the United States and, albeit slower, elsewhere. These hotels, that trace their ancestry back to the opening of Marriott's *Residence Inn* in 1974, are normally defined as hotels where guests stay for more than five nights and that do not offer ancillary services such as bars, restaurants and porterage. It is estimated that up to 20% of United States hotel stays are over five days and extended stay hotels account for most of this type of accommodation (240,000 rooms). While not all are regular 'commuters' and not all use the low-cost air services to travel to their accommodation, many do.

5 Finance and ownership

From a policy perspective, while there are good reasons to ensure that adequate transport is available to facilitate economic development, there are market imperfections that can impede this happening. One serious set of constraints in most countries is that associated with planning requirements. These can delay the construction of a facility and affect its design and operations. We will not deal with these issues here, because they vary considerably between countries, but rather focus on issues of finance and efficient operations. Financing can pose particular problems in poorer countries, or even regions within more prosperous nations if they do not have an adequate tax base, or access to more sophisticated money markets.

Airports are relatively expensive build and, because of their monopoly status in many locations, are often not operated efficiently. To reduce the X-inefficiency, there have been moves in many countries to make airport operators more commercially oriented. The national approaches aimed at injecting more commercial pressures into the provision of airport services have varied. Much of the interest that is now emerging is either the privatization of some aspects of airport activity or engaging the private sector in some partnership arrangement with the state. In part this is because an airport is effectively a composite entity comprised of units offering a variety of services – land access, parking, concessions, terminals, runways, ground handling, fire and response units, security, etc. Commercialization does not have to be applied to all these activities, and may be pursued in a piece-meal way if politics or economics dictate.

Approaches differ according to the state of the local air transport market that is, in turn, often linked to the stage in economic development of the region concerned. For example, airports can vary in terms of their potential revenue flow from different sources – e.g. slot fees and concession – and this can affect the degree of privatization or deregulation that is possible and the form it is most likely to take.

Much depends on the state of the regional air transport market. The forecasts of relatively slow longer term growth in air traffic in and between the developed countries (e.g. estimated at about 3.6% a year to 2025 within North America, 3.4% within Europe and 4.5% between North America and Europe) means that their major airports will increasingly become dependent on commercial or non-aeronautical revenues to enhance their revenue stream. This in turn can pose problems in terms of regulation as has already been seen in the debates over the imposition of the price-capping regime used in the United Kingdom.

While still relatively small, the protected growth of many air markets involving regions of developing countries offers the potential for increased airside revenue in situations where there are potentially fewer social constraints involving such things as noise and land-take on building additional capacity or where there is already adequate capacity. The scope for raising significant commercial income is much less, however, because of lower initial traffic bases. It also suggests, though, that the regulatory regime overseeing a privatized airport system needs to be less sophisticated because it only has to deal with airside issues, making the potential for various forms of regulatory capture smaller.

The problem for regions of the poorest developing countries, however, is that even though their air traffic flows may in aggregate be growing, this is from a low base and they still seldom generate sufficient revenue to cover the full costs of operations. Airports are essentially decreasing cost entities for which cost recovery can be difficult, especially in a situation where there is competition from other airports. This makes pure privatization options less tenable and the need for outside assistance from aid agencies or from government more relevant. Private/public partnerships offer another alternative [23].

The wide variety of circumstances around the world has led to a diversity of approaches to commercialization of airports. Some have involved complete divestiture of former state assets to the private sector, albeit with some oversight of how the airport is operated, but in other instances the withdrawal of the state has been less complete.

The management contract approach retains government control, but involves contracting out specified elements of airport services – parking, hotels, retail concessions, etc. – for periods of time. This normally involves some form of auction. The system is in line with the notion of 'competition for the market'. Long term contracting involves giving over the operational side of an airport, sometimes including investment commitments in additional capacity, for an extended period with the authorities retaining a degree of strategic control. The financing required normally entails bringing inspecialized international companies with the expertise to manage an airport, or system of airports, together with finance houses that can provide the necessary support for large scale service activities. These types of concessions are widespread in South America, where local expertise and finance is limited, but there is reluctance for the state to divest itself of aviation assets.

Many developed countries have also pursued similar philosophies when expanding the involvement of private enterprise, but falling short of the complete divestiture [24]. Many United States airports have adopted various concessionary schemes – for example Boston, Pittsburgh and Reagan National Airport, Washington have entered into concessionaire agreements, for the entire operations at Pittsburgh and for specific terminal buildings at the other airports.

At Chicago O'Hare airport, parking has been contracted out, and the Port Authority of New York and New Jersey, that own a number of airports, has a variety of agreements covering such things as the operation of terminal buildings and the supply of heating and cooling at some of its facilities. There is also a tradition in the United States of significant airline involvement in providing check-in facilities and baggage systems.

Complete privatization of major airports is uncommon, although increasing. In most cases, there is concern that a privately owned airport will exercise its monopoly power to extract rent from customers. The challenges are to device and operationalize appropriate regulatory regimes to monitor and direct these large companies in the public interest – often price-capping is deployed. The on-going debates about full privatization concern such things as whether single airport, or as with the United Kingdom's BAA, systems of airports, should be privatized and when they are privatized what should be regulated; should it be all airport activities or just those directly aviation related?

In their overview of various governance options, Carney and Mew [25] focus correctly on the government being involved in both seeking to improve the efficiency of their airports and trying to direct the gains to particular groups rather than leaving management with full autonomy in their actions. This involves complexities that, while common to businesses in developed countries, are unfamiliar in many parts of the world. As a result, this has added to the growth in international firms specializing in airport management, including ownership, to allow the development of common, best-practice methods of operation while at the same time being innovative in creating bespoke models for different circumstances.

6 Retaining air services

Airlines are by definition mobile, and simply attracting an airline service to an airport does not guarantee that it will continue services or that it will always offer the same range of services. In the world of deregulated airline markets, the commitment of carriers to serve particular airports is governed by the profitability of the services that it offers. There are some fixed costs of starting a new service and of withdrawing there are stranded costs, but these are relatively small. Airlines can lease or rent most things required to operate a service, including planes, crew, catering, slots, gates, space on reservation systems, baggage handling and check in facilities. Withdraw of a service can also mean transfer of assets if they are owned by an airline, or the assets being leased to another airline.

In contrast to this flexibility, industry and individuals seek continuity of services in their decision-making. When deciding where to locate, a company usually commits considerable sums that are not fully recoverable in the short to medium term, or at least not without considerable discounting. The sunk costs elements are even greater when there is specialized plant and equipment involved. Similarly, with individuals, when selecting a place to live consideration is given to the quality of transport services in the area and the larger accessibility of the area in national and international terms. Moving from an area, particularly one that has gone into an economic downturn can be costly to individuals that have bought, or taken out long-leases on homes and can have serious social implications for families that have to abandon personal ties. In effect, airlines are much more flexible in terms of the services that they offer than many of the businesses and households that make use of their services.

This problem is compounded because the competitive scheduled airline service is highly unstable. Figure 1 shows the operating margins in the main airline markets of the world. Elementary economic theory tells us that when there are no fixed-costs then competitive bargaining between suppliers and customers will ensure that prices are kept to the minimum level that that do not allow suppliers to recover all costs over the long term. When there are no fixed costs, the marginal cost of meeting customer demand represents the entire costs of production. The problems come when there are fixed costs. In this case markets can be very unstable.

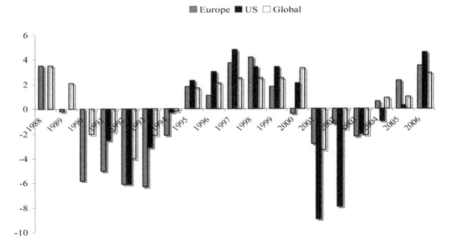

Figure 1: Operating margins of airlines (1988–2006).

Notes: (i) A lack of a bar indicates a missing observation and not a zero operating margin, (ii) memberships of the various reporting bodies vary over time and thus the reported margins reflect the associated carriers at the time of reporting.

Sources: Boeing Commercial Airplane, Association of European Airlines, Air Transport Association of America, International Air Transport Association.

The traditional view of fixed costs was developed when the bricks, steel and mortar of industrial plants had to be paid for. The world has changed, and with service industries, and especially those like airlines that provide scheduled services, the fixed costs are somewhat different. While airlines do use expensive hardware, as we have seemed, this does not imply that this in itself imposes a fixed cost. Fixed costs for airlines take an entirely different form.

An airline is committed to a particular scheduled service some six months or so before the flight – it is committed to have a plane, crew, fuel, gates, landing and take-off slots, etc. In deregulated market they engage in price discrimination, charging passengers different fares to try to extract as much revenue as possible. In general, this means that lower fares are offered initially when a fight is some way off because leisure travellers are willing to pay less for a seat and are more flexible in their scheduling and will seek lower fares if available. They are caught early by the airline. Towards the time of take-off, fares rise as last minute travellers, often business travellers, seek seats. These people are less sensitive to fares because meeting a last minute business deadline can make or break a deal, and tax deductions are normally allowed for the offsetting of higher fares.

The problem is that with a fixed schedule in a competitive market, the various airlines set take-off times for each destination at about the same time. This leads to intense competition to fill seats and forces fares down to the levels that do not allow all the costs of individual's services to be met. It is worth filing a seat once it is there with anyone willing to pay for the additional costs of handling.[14]

Airlines have sought to minimize this problem in a variety of ways. Many offer frequent flier programmes to retain customers, seek to control information and booking systems, focus on routes where, either because they are new or for some institutional reason, they legally have a degree of market power, try to find ways of getting state subsidies, concentrate services on major 'fortress' hubs where they control gates and slots, form cartels as strategic alliances so as to widen their market presence and reduce costs, and others seek to limit competition by keeping costs low – the 'low cost business model'. For a time these policies may work but, for example, fortress hubs have proved vulnerable to point-to-point services and as load factors have increased so the values of frequent flier miles have diminished – there are simply fewer services they can be redeemed on.

The inability of airlines as a whole to recover their full costs makes continuity of service provision uncertain, and particularly so during any period of economic recession or slow growth. The low-cost business model has been touted as a possible solution to this and it is true that in Europe there has been significant regional economic development around major low-cost airports such as Frankfurt Hahn served by Ryanair. But, the low-cost model itself is not stable and there have been numerous failed low-cost airlines. Table 3 gives examples in Europe covering a relatively short period. While Ryanair and Southwest (in the United States) have prospered, they enjoyed clear first-mover advantages in their respective markets.

There have been efforts on the part of industry to ensure continuity of services from regional airports. In Europe, for example, Chambers of Commerce such as that in Strasbourg have sought to subsidize services but have run foul of European Union laws regarding the use of public money. In the United States, direct private sector has been more active in retaining air services.[15]

Table 3: European low-cost carriers that ceased to exist (2003 to 2005).*

Aeris	BuzzAway	Hellas Jet
Agent	Dream Air	Hop
Air Bosnia	Duo	Jet Magic
Air Andalucia	Europe DutchBird	Jetgreen
Air Catalunya	EastJet	JetsSky
Europe Air Exel	EU Jet	JetX
Air Freedom	Europe Exel Aviation Group	Low Fare Jet
Europe Air	Fairline Austria	Maersk Air
Air Littoral	Fly Eco	Now
Air Luxor	Fly West	Silesian Air
Air Madrid	Flying Finn	Skynet Airlines
Air Polonia	Free Airways	Spirit Of Balkan
Air Wales	Fresh Aer	Swedline Express
Airlib Express	Germania Express	V Bird
BasiqAir	GetJet Poland	VolareWeb
BerlinJet	Go Fly	White Eagle
Bexx Air	Goodjet	Windjet

* Most of these airlines operated for a period and then went into bankruptcy. Some such
as Go Fly and BuzzAway merged with successful low-cost airlines. In a few cases, the
airline was registered but never offered actual services.

7 Conclusions

Much of the modern world, and particularly so in the high income, market
oriented economies, is based on mobility and accessibility. There are few cases
of significant economic development in regions that are spatially remote and are
not tied into modern transport networks. The development of an airport in a
region is not a panacea that will suddenly bring economic prosperity. It has to
attract airlines' services, and services that are likely to be durable over the
foreseeable future. To do that the region has to have intrinsic features that can
be exploited by air access – airlines essentially seek to exploit these local
advantages by moving the people and goods associated with them.

What we have argued here is that it is inadequate to simply consider the
airport infrastructure in isolation when assessing the role of airport investment in
regional economic development. The normal economic impact work conducted
as part of the initial planning of an airport is seldom adequate, particularly when
the role of air transport has changed so much in recent years. The way an airport
is financed and operated affects the nature and quality of air services that it
provides. Simply having a set of buildings and a runway of itself, may prove
ineffective if the financial structure does not allow adequate maintenance and
there is no incentive for management to operate the airport efficiently. Further,
no airport can be treated in isolation from the airlines that use it. The economic

market for airline services is a complicated one and one that is prone to serious instabilities.

Notes

1. Air navigation systems are required for traffic control and advice but these are more akin to traffic management (signals, signs, etc.) on roads than the roads themselves.
2. There is also a tendency when private airports have their returns regulated for them to over-invest. This Averch–Johnson effect [1] is commonly seemed as 'gold-plating' by airlines.
3. A survey of the literature on regional economic growth theories is contained in Button [8].
4. These may be thought of as producing an upward shift in a region's production function rather than just a movement along it.
5. Button and his co-workers [15] found that in the United States a city with a major hub-airport had, on average, an extra 12,000 high technology goods in the region.
6. There is also the issue of the extent to which migrants remain at a gateway and 'push-out' existing workers that are forced to migrate internally to other parts of the country.
7. This is an estimate and includes short-term migration. The United Kingdom Office of National Statistics (web site: http://www.statistics.gov.uk/) provides periodic data on migration but given the flexibility of the European labour market, this only offers broad approximations of trends. For example, it is weak regarding duration of employment and on the movement of self-employed labour.
8. In the past, there has been considerable interest in the role of transport in facilitating labour migration, for example in terms of examining the role of shipping development in the forced migration of slaves from Africa to the Americas and of convicts from the United Kingdom to Australia, and of voluntary migration as facilitated by such as the transcontinental American railroads.
9. Migration is normally defined as individuals living outside their county of birth for more than a year. This data misses illegal migration, although it is sometimes estimated, and a number of groups, such as students, who may live in a country for an extended period but are not considered immigrants.
10. Low airfares and services to secondary airports in Europe have stimulated, for example, an extensive migration of retirees from cooler countries such as the United Kingdom to Spain, Portugal, France and Italy. For example, in 2005, 224,841 British people were registered in Spain, 136,766 having an EU residence card, and some 75,000–100,000 were estimated by the Spanish government to reside there.
11. Saxenian's study [19] provides details of labour structures in California and their travel to and from home.
12. Overall there are over 400 million long distance business trips, 16% of all business trips, made a year in the US, but many of these cannot be defined as commuting since they are irregular and with individuals going to a diversity of destinations. Of trips of 100 miles or more, 13% were made by air in 2001, with an average distance of 2,080 miles.
13. Most studies of United States long-distance commuting normally define it as commutes of over 90 minutes or 50 miles. Air travel makes little impact on most trips of this length but cuts in for much longer commutes of several hundred miles or more.
14. This generic problem is seen to exist when there is an 'empty core' [26, 27].
15. In Wichita, Kansas, 400 businesses raised $7.2 million to attract carriers. Air Tran started operations in May 2002 with services to Atlanta and Chicago's Midway airport. The agreement included up to $3.0 million to cover losses in its first year and

$1.5 million in the second. Similarly, Pensacola, Florida raised $2.1 million from 319 businesses to attract Air Tran while companies and individuals in Stockton, California bought $800,000 of prepaid tickets to attract American West.

References

[1] Averch, H. & Johnson, L.L., Behavior of the firm under regulatory constraint. *American Economic Review*, **52(5)**, pp. 1052–1069, 1962.

[2] Kaldor, N., The case for regional policies. *Scottish Journal of Economics*, **17(3)**, pp. 337–348, 1970.

[3] Lucas, R.E., Making a miracle. *Econometrica*, **61(2)**, pp. 251–272, 1993.

[4] Romer, P.M., Endogenous technical change. *Journal of Political Economy*, **98(5)**, pp. S71–S102, 1990.

[5] Romer, P.M., The origins of endogenous growth. *Journal of Economic Perspectives*, **8(1)**, pp. 3–22, 1994.

[6] Barro, R.J. & Sala-i-Martin, X., Convergence across states and regions. *Brookings Papers on Economic Activity*, **1**, pp. 107–182, 1991.

[7] Barro, R.J & Sala-i-Martin, X., Convergence. *Journal of Political Economy*, **100(5)**, pp. 223–251, 1992.

[8] Button, K.J., The economist's perspective on regional endogenous development. *Regional Endogenous Development*, eds. R. Stimson & R. Stough, Cheltenham, Gloucestershire: Edward Elgar, 2008.

[9] Williams, G.A., *Comparison of Airports in the EU*, Bedfordshire, UK: Department of Air Transport, Cranfield University, 2005.

[10] Aschauer, D.A., Does public capital crowd out private capital? *Journal of Monetary Economics*, **24(2)**, pp. 171–188, 1989.

[11] Button, K.J., Infrastructure investment, endogenous growth and economic convergence. *Annals of Regional Science*, **32(1)**, pp. 145–162, 1998.

[12] Green, R.K., Airports and economic development, *Real Estate Economics*, **35(1)**, pp. 91–112, 2007.

[13] Butler, S.E. & Kiernan, L.J., *Measuring the Regional Economic Significance of Airports*, Washington, DC: Office of Airport Planning and Programming, Federal Aviation Administration, 1992.

[14] Debbage, K.G., Airport runway slots: Limits to growth. *Annals of Tourism Research*, **29(19)**, pp. 933–951, 2002.

[15] Button, K.J., Lall, S., Stough, R. & Trice, M., High-technology employment and hub airports. *Journal of Air Transport Management*, **5(1)**, pp. 53–59, 1999.

[16] Button, K.J. & Taylor, S.Y., International air transport and economic development. *Journal of Air Transport Management*, **6(4)**, pp. 209–222, 2000.

[17] Button, K.J. & Vega, H., The effects of air transport on the movement of labour. *GeoJournal*, **71(1)**, pp. 67–81, 2008.

[18] Abella, M.I., *Skilled Labour Migration from Developing Countries: Analysis of Impact and Policy Issues*, Geneva: International Labour Organisation, International Labour Office, DFID Paper Series, 2002.

[19] Saxenian, A., *Local and Global Networks of Immigrant Professionals in Silicon Valley*, San Francisco: Public Policy Institute of California, 2002.

[20] Michaels, D., 'Ethnic' routes, growth market for airlines: Cheap travel for immigrants. *Wall Street Journal*, 7(March), p. A1, 2007.

[21] United Kingdom Civil Aviation Authority, *No-frills Carriers: Revolution or Evolution? A Study by the Civil Aviation Authority*, London: Civil Aviation Authority, 2006.

[22] Portes, A., Global villagers: The rise of transnational communities. *The American Prospect*, March–April, pp. 74–77, 1996.

[23] Button, K.J., Air transport infrastructure in developing countries: Privatization and deregulation. *Aviation Infrastructure Performance: A Study in Comparative Political Economy*, eds. C. Winston & G. de Rus, Washington, DC: Brookings Institution, pp. 193–221, 2008.

[24] Button, K.J., The Implications of the commercialization of air transport infrastructure. *The Economics of Airline Institutions, Operations and Marketing 2*, ed. D. Lee, Oxford: Elsevier, pp. 171–192, 2007.

[25] Carney, M. & Mew, K., Airport governance reform: a strategic management perspective. *Journal of Air Transport Management*, **9(2)**, pp. 221–232, 2003.

[26] Button, K.J., Liberalising European aviation: Is there an empty core problem? *Journal of Transport Economics and Policy*, **30(3)**, pp. 275–291, 1996.

[27] Button, K.J., Does the theory of the 'core' explain why airlines fail to cover their long-run costs of capital? *Journal of Air Transport Management*, **9(1)**, pp. 5–14, 2003.

2

Development of regional airports in EU

M. Nadia Postorino
University 'Mediterranea' of Reggio Calabria, Italy

Abstract

A suitable development of regional airports in large areas, such as continental areas, can be obtained if there exist appropriate policies addressed to achieve this goal. In the specific case of the European Union, some specific programmes at European level, such as the Single European Sky and the Trans-European Network programmes, will have many implications for the development of regional airports as well as the relationships between regional airports and low-cost air carriers. Regional airports can play an important role to reduce the congestion peaks at main airports, particularly in the light of an integrated transport network where many modes coexist and can integrate or substitute each other. Particularly, high-speed rail can improve the airport accessibility by increasing its catchment area or represent an alternative to the air mode.

Keywords: airport capacity; high-speed rail; low-cost air carriers; regional airports; SESAR; TEN-T.

1 Introduction

In the last years, the air transport system has grown quickly and the planning policies had to be adjusted to guarantee a suitable development of both air services (as courses, frequencies, fares and airport services) and infrastructures (as airports and land transport access facilities).

The deregulation process, started in 1978 in the USA with the Deregulation Act, and then in Europe with the 'Packet for aviation liberalization', has led to a further reorganization in the air field and such a process is still in progress.

The relatively recent foundation of the European Union (EU) has given rise to a set of problems concerning the Air Traffic Control (ATC) system along routes that are some of the most congested in the world, mainly due to the lack of homogenous procedures among the several European Nations. To this aim, the EU has started an ambitious programme to create a Single European Sky (SESAR project) in order to have a good ATC along the routes and to identify Air Traffic Management (ATM) policies able to improve capacity and develop an efficient and sustainable European air transport system by maintaining a high level of safety. ATM environmental efficiency is one of the key objectives of the SESAR programme as the EU gives a great importance to the reduction of the environmental impact of aviation, in particular greenhouse gas emissions and noise. At the same time, safety is the other important goal to be achieved: in fact, although flying is one of the safest travel mode, as existing technical systems reach the limits of their capacity, the risk of accidents grows, thus making crucial the development of a new generation of ATM systems able to satisfy the needs of safety and efficiency of flight operations, in the air as well as on the ground.

Congestion and delays at the airports are another important problem, and environmental considerations on the really crowded European continent often prevent the larger airports from expanding. In fact, most important airports are quite near to cities and produce important negative effects due to both air services (as noise and pollution) and airport land accessibility (as road congestion). As air traffic in Europe is expected to increase substantially in the next 20 years, the above problems are also expected to worsen if suitable policies for a sustainable development are not implemented. Furthermore, as collected data show, the cost of the European ATC system increases as air traffic increases, and hence, all things being the same, also costs are expected to grow in the future.

In the USA, the harmonization of the aviation ATC procedures overcomes the EU problems, but the system is congested as well. In particular, the territorial extension of the USA as unique country and the significant development of the aviation sector with respect to alternative land systems (as railways services) have made the air transport system the most used in the country. Low-cost carriers have given a further impulse to its diffusion, thus making the air transport system the most preferred means of transport to move within the USA.

The great interest for regional airport development both in the EU and the USA is then mainly due to their potential role in reducing the congestion along the main used routes and also reducing the negative impacts at the hub airport nodes, both for the air transport users and the overall community.

The use of regional airports has many advantages: (1) satisfactory airport capacity availability; (2) opportunity to promote the socio-economic development of decentralized areas and regions; (3) reduction of negative impacts due to the less traffic levels; (4) development of a spreader air service network.

In this light, many policies have been introduced by the EU, specifically addressed to promote the re-valuation of regional airports in the several EU nations. As stated by the European Commission (EC), 'Regional airports are important to the development of an integrated European air transport network. In this respect, it would be desirable to unlock existing latent capacity at regional airports provided that Member States respect Community legal instruments relating to state aids. Global Navigation Satellite Systems could play a significant role for increasing capacity and flexibility of operations at those airports without increasing the cost of local infrastructure. Member States should endeavour to improve the accessibility of such airports by rail and road to allow them to act as reliever airports.' ('An action plan for airport capacity, efficiency and safety in Europe', Brussels, Jan 2007.)

At the same time, the continuous development of low-cost air carriers has given a further impulse to the re-valuation of regional airports. In fact, low-cost air carriers prefer to use regional airports for many reasons as follows: reduced aviation costs at the airport, competitive taxi and turn-around times, availability of airport capacity due to low traffic congestion and so on. Furthermore, they can also benefit from start-up, within the rules of compatibility established by the Articles 87–89 of the EC Treaties and the Community guidelines on financing of airports and start-up aid to airlines departing from regional airports. Particularly, Article 87(3)(a) and (c) apply in relation to undertakings established or investing in disadvantaged regions. The Guidelines specifically refer to its application in relation to aid for undertakings financing the building of a hangar in such regions. However, Article 87(3)(c) cannot be used to justify operating aids (except the case where an undertaking is established in an eligible region and the measure counterbalances particular difficulties).

To summarize, the EC recognizes the importance of regional airports to develop an integrated European air transport network because their existing latent capacity can reduce the congestion peaks at main airports; anyway, in order to design an effective air transport network the EC also recommends the improvement of their accessibility (rail and road access).

Thus, the use of regional airports can bring many advantages not only to the air companies, airports and users, but also to the whole community both in terms of social benefits (increased accessibility from decentralized or peripheral regions) and potential economic expansion.

In the following, after an overview of the European main transport policies, addressed to assure quick and easy trips within the EU (Sections 2), the main challenges of the European airports in terms of capacity, charges and state aids are considered (Section 3); the main relationships between regional airports and low-cost air carriers in the European context are also summarized (Section 4); and finally, some main conclusions are discussed (Section 5).

2 Main transport policies to assure easy mobility within EU

As well known, the EU is a relatively recent institution: born in 1950 with only six nations, today is formed by 25 nations within the European continent, following a significant enlargement in 2004 (Figure 1). Furthermore, two nations (Bulgaria and Romania) have already signed the Accession Treaty while another two (Croatia and Turkey), and several others, have requested for the EU membership.

Figure 1: The European Union.

The progressive enlargement of the EU has posed many questions concerning the way towards the harmonization of procedures and policies, mainly in the field of air transport where the integration of the existing control systems is crucial for the safety and efficiency of the air navigation.

Many transport policies have been implemented in order to define a Trans-European Transport Network (TEN-T) thus enabling European citizens to move along the EU in a quick and efficient way.

For the air transport system, key elements to meet the goals of safety and efficiency can be identified in the following: (1) better effective use of existing airport capacity; (2) improvement of the airport environmental capacity as well as the planning framework for new airport infrastructure; (3) integration among several transport modes (co-modality) to assure fast, efficient and safe trips; (4) development and implementation of cost-efficient technological solutions.

Two main transport policies are here discussed, concerning the air traffic development and the fast railway system. Following the EC design of an integrated, co-modal, spread transport system, they are related to each other because air transport and railway systems are competitive on some routes but complementary on some others. Improvement of co-modality is one of the basic targets recommended by the EC that can also be achieved thanks to available Community funds.

Before discussing the implication of competition-complementarities between high-speed lines and air transport, an overview of the airport capacity problem is presented and then the already recalled SESAR project and the Community multiannual TEN-T programme are briefly described, with particular reference to the implication for the development of regional airports.

2.1 The airport capacity problems

The airport capacity is an important matter for the EC, as it will not be able to meet the demand in the next future and then it could be the most constraining factor on the overall air transport chain. Furthermore, new problems concerning the sustainability of airports, particularly the airport noise management, will further constrain the capacity following the concept of environmental capacity as 'the capacity of the receiving environment, both human and non-human, to tolerate the impacts of airport activity' (Upham *et al.* [1, 2]). Given that acoustic impacts are the most relevant for the airport activities, the airport acoustical capacity is also defined as 'the maximum number of aircraft movements, per RWY direction, within a specified lapse of time, generating a noise level at most equal to the one prescribed by laws for a particular area'. Then, aircraft noise is a major constraint to airport development.

To overcome the environmental constraints, noiseless aircraft are now operating to meet the government requirements of improving noise climate around airports (e.g. Directive 2002/30/EC), even if many airlines continue to use old noisy aircraft. Anyway, as air traffic is expected to increase significantly in the next future, this measure will soon be ineffective and then noise operating restrictions on aircraft should not be applied as a first alternative, but only after consideration of the benefits to be gained from other elements.

The Balanced Approach to Noise (as fixed during the ICAO Assembly in 2001) identifies an international approach to tackle airport aircraft noise problems in an environmentally reactive and economically responsible way. It includes four main elements:

- reduction of noise at source;
- land-use planning and management;
- noise abatement operational procedures;
- noise operating restrictions on aircraft.

Then, both the increase in demand and the restrictive constraints to guarantee environmental sustainability can decrease the efficiency of airports, often considered as one of the engines for the economic growth of a region, thus undermining the overall competitiveness of the European economy.

As recent traffic estimates report, over 60 European airports will be heavily congested and the top 20 airports will be saturated at least 8–10 hours per day by 2025, if any efficient policy to increase the capacity levels is undertaken. The worsening of the available capacity levels, mainly at hub airports, has serious impacts on the overall efficiency of the European air transport industry. In fact, critical congestion at airports means not only that airline schedules cannot be assured, but also that environmental and safety costs increase.

The actions that can be undertaken to overcome these problems can be identified in the more efficient use of the existing runways and the support for new infrastructures as well as a suitable balance between market-driven solutions (as market mechanisms for slot allocation) and regulatory measures (as Single European Sky and airport safety management). In any case, aviation security must be always assured whichever the actions undertaken to increase airport capacity.

In this overall perspective, regional airports are a key element to the development of an integrated European air transport network, because they can benefit from existing unused capacity and, if well linked to the main land transport connections (both roads and railways), can be a suitable alternative to more congested main airports.

Furthermore, they can overcome the slot assignment problems, very crucial for coordinated airports. In the current EC Regulation – Article 2(a) [3], a 'slot' is defined as 'the permission given by a coordinator in accordance with this Regulation to use the full range of airport infrastructure necessary to operate an air service at a coordinated airport on a specific date and time for the purpose of landing or take-off as allocated by a coordinator in accordance with this Regulation'. According to the Regulation, Community airports with a serious loss in capacity should be designated as 'coordinated airports' on the basis of objective criteria after a capacity analysis has been conducted, taking into account environmental constraints at the airport itself. In other words, in a coordinated airport time windows are assigned by a coordinator to airlines for taking-off/landing (slot allocation); so, air carriers can access airport facilities for landing and taking-off at specific dates and times for the duration of the period for which the permission is granted. Only emergency and humanitarian flights as well as government flights are excluded.

According to Article 3 of the EC Slot Regulation, in any specific time period coordinated airports identify the number of slots that are offered and they are divided into arrival and departure slots. Such a partition takes into account the impact of other operational constraints, such as aircraft size and capacity, and maximum possible passenger throughput. The slot management and assignment can have significant consequences on the capacity of coordinated airports, and such a process should be based on assignment criteria inspired by transparency and unbiased principles.

In congested airports, delays in arrival/departure of aircraft means that slot availability is no more assured and then delays can extend to several flights with increased costs both for users and airlines. Delays predictability is then crucial both for airlines and airports in their operation management. Generally, airlines consider in their schedule a 'buffer time' to take into account unexpected delays in arriving or departing aircraft. Anyway, this enlarged time means also an inefficient use of the time resource and then a worsening in the overall airport capacity. As an example, 5 minutes of buffer time means a cost of about €1000 million in the use of airline and airport resources.

In terms of slot allocation systems, at airports where capacity limits exist, a slot coordination committee allocates slots on the basis of some criteria, mainly on the basis of 'grandfathering' rights. It means that slots are assigned to incumbent airlines according to their prior use of these slots. This method has been strongly criticized and some countries have introduced the rule 'use it or lose it', that is airlines lose their slot if they do not use it above 80% of the time. This measure tries to avoid that incumbent airlines can take strategic action in order to discourage the entry of new competitors. The 'grandfathering' slot allocation system perpetuates the market presence of an air carrier at an airport without ensuring that the air carrier will use them in the best way (i.e. offer competitive services to the largest possible number of passengers).

2.2 The Single European Sky (SESAR) project

As introduced before, the SESAR project is aimed at designing and implementing a single ATM Master Plan (including technology and operational aspects), based on the Interoperability Regulation; in fact, air transport is international by nature, so an ATM global interoperability is needed, for economic and technical reasons, and above all for safety reasons.

The SESAR programme consists of two phases:

- the definition phase (2005–2007);
- the implementation phase (2008–2020).

The definition phase has been designed and co-funded by both the EC and Eurocontrol (the European organization for air navigation safety) in order to define a European ATM Master Plan. In turn, such a plan consists of:

- a technology roadmap, with target dates for development and introduction of specific systems;
- a proposed system architecture;
- a detailed funding and implementation plan.

The implementation phase will consist of two steps:

- during the first step (2008–2013) the technologies underlying the new generation of systems should be developed together with functional enhancements in areas such as evolution of automated support tools and task-sharing between ground and aircraft;
- during the second step (2014–2020) the new systems will be used at large scale as well as their enhanced functional capacities. It is expected that the new ATM system will treble current capacity, increase safety by at least a factor of ten and will have an operating cost significantly less than today.

In order to extend the potential of a single sky in a larger environment, SESAR is thought as a worldwide project. In fact, many agreements are expected with third countries and Partner States. Cooperation agreements with third countries will help to synchronize the SESAR technological and operational choices with other modernization initiatives. On the other hand, Partner States will be invited to become members of the SESAR Joint Undertaking, to contribute to the technological programme, as well as other potential Single Sky activities.

To reach the goal of a Single European Sky, the European technical and organizational infrastructure needs to evolve; the main aspects involved in the identification of a Single European Sky, particularly in what concerns the European ATM, are as follows:

- the separation of regulatory activities from service provision, and the possibility of cross-border ATM services;
- the integration of airspace into Functional Airspace Blocks (FABs), defined in line with operational traffic flows and no longer constrained by national borders;
- the crucial role of the EC in setting common rules and standards, covering a wide range of issues such as flight data exchanges and telecommunications.

The SESAR programme is also addressed to develop new technologies aiming at further increasing the safety and efficiency of airport operations. In particular, both goals are linked to the separation between aircraft and the relating control devices that can help in assuring and monitoring such a separation.

Separation between aircraft depends on wake vortexes that in turn depend on the aircraft dimensions. As well known, the increase in separation will increase the safety level, but will decrease the airport capacity. Then, an optimal agreement between safety and capacity exigencies has to be achieved. New wake vortex prediction and detection devices will enable to safely reduce separation minima between aircraft while new generations of airport airside management tools will enable the optimization of ground movements. Finally, new sensors will enable remote tower operations. Then, the final goal to achieve both safety and efficiency in airports can be obtained.

Furthermore, Advanced-Surface Movement Ground Control Systems (A-SMGCS) surveillance and control functions should be implemented throughout European airports, since safety for the aerodrome airside includes not only the infrastructure but also operations and management.

As known, a SMGCS can be used not only to control the ground circulation in order to guarantee suitable safety standards, but also to optimally manage the ground movement (Postorino et al. [4]), that is by reducing possible excessive spaces among aircraft and addressing the moving vehicles along the best path in order to optimize the whole system in terms of capacity. An A-SMGCS must also answer to requirements such as surveillance, routing, guidance and control functions.

Finally, to conclude this section a brief overview about Galileo is needed. Galileo is the future European satellite navigation system, planned to be operational by 2013 and is to be included in the Trans-European Network (TEN) (see Section 2.3) as a major technological project for the industry. It will be formed by a global constellation of 30 satellites, distributed over three planes in medium Earth orbit, and ground stations providing information concerning the positioning of users in many sectors. It is expected to give a great contribution to the development of technologies, organization methods and industrial components which can ensure the safety and fluidity of air transport in the next 20 years.

As the White Paper [5] (Part 4 'Managing the Globalisation of Traffic') indicates, the Galileo programme represents a key need for global transport programming and for removing the European dependence on GPS (USA) and GLONASS (Russia) satellite navigation systems. Actually, Galileo is aimed at ensuring interoperability with the previous two systems, but it is also an independent system, in the sense that it will not be subjected to any limitation as introduced in the other two systems because of military considerations.

Galileo will support Intelligent Traffic Systems, mainly in order to provide navigational functions, real time information to users and optimized control to urban and interurban transportation. Positive impacts of the provided navigation and information services are expected, particularly: decreased travel times, increased capacity of transport links and increased safety.

The availability of an additional satellite constellation offers significant benefits to aviation in terms of improved performance and robustness, particularly resistance to unplanned interferences, greater availability of satellites, robustness to control segment failures, improved availability and continuity.

2.3 Trans-European Network Transport project

The first plan of a TENs was born at the end of the 1980s, with the idea of making available a free movement of goods, persons and services among the Europe. This is possible only if the various regions and national networks that form the single market are suitably linked by modern and efficient infrastructure. The construction of a TEN-T (Figure 2) is an important element for the economic growth and the creation of employment in the EU (European Commission [6, 7]).

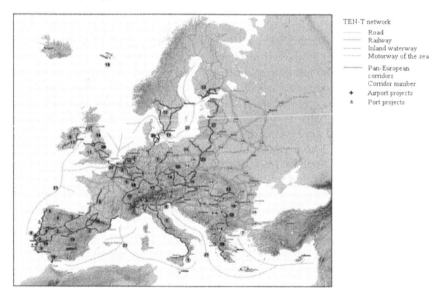

Figure 2: Trans-European Transport Network (TEN-T).
Source: European Commission (ec.europa.eu/ten/transport/maps/axes_en.htm).

Furthermore, as transport has always been a key element to guarantee economic and social cohesion, the identification of a TEN is crucial for the creation of the internal market. Given that the EU process towards the unification is still in progress, it is important to establish the interconnection and interoperability of national networks as well as access to such networks.

In this context, airports are not merely air transportation infrastructures, but rather they should be considered as inter-modal nodes in a larger multimodal transportation network. Actually, for the vast majority of travellers, airports are multimodal interchange nodes. Similarly, many freight transporters are using air transportation as one of the links of their trip chain and, again, airports are serving as modal interchange points.

As airports are generally located far from city centres, passenger or freight movements involving air travel require the use of other transportation modes to reach the airport. Generally, two secondary trips can be identified: the first one to access the airport to initiate the air transportation component of the overall trip, and the second one to move from the airport at the end of a flight to the final destination. In that sense, all airports are multimodal interchange nodes. Anyway, more in-depth analyses can prove different levels of complexity in the interchange role of an airport. In fact, in some cases the trip to/from the airport is simply the access and egress from the air transportation network, as air travel is the primary mode.   In other cases, there may be more than one primary mode (e.g. local transportation to an airport, a flight, an intercity rail journey and local transportation to the destination).

Furthermore, the growth of low-cost air services at some secondary airports has significant implications for the local surface transportation. Many of the airports used by low-cost carriers are generally far from the final destination city (e.g. Frankfurt/Hahn is about 100 kilometres from Frankfurt). In a very small number of cases there are limited local train services but, in general, access and egress is by road transportation. This can lead to congestion on routes that do not have the capacity to cope with the additional traffic flows, cause road damage on pavements not originally designed for such flows and impose an environmental burden on areas that were previously relatively quiet.

In order to speed up the integration progress among the several EU nations and to improve accessibility, the EC has provided a large amount of specific funds that, together with the Structural and Cohesion Funds, could be used as leverage for national funding. Furthermore, specific attention has been addressed to cross-border projects in order to obtain a more effective integration among neighbouring nations.

The TEN-T actions are periodically revised to take into account new exigencies and projects already finished. Main important corridors have to link both Northern and Southern European regions as well as Eastern and Western countries. Together with the land network extension, both in terms of road and railway infrastructures, also the 'Motorways of the Sea' are key targets within the TEN-T framework. They should ensure regular, high-capacity ferry routes between the main ports in the EU, in order to improve the efficiency and reliability of freight transport and then provide suitable alternatives for congested land routes on roads. Their benefits are expected in the economic and social fields in terms of improved cohesion between the involved countries: enhanced accessibility; reduction in transport costs and times; improvement of quality; creation of employment; access to new markets.

One of the most important consequences of the TEN-T actions is the expected increase in the accessibility among the several EU nations and, inside the same nations, among regions. Conventional accessibility indicators measure the total effect of both geographical location (periphery vs. centre) and quality of transport provided by the transport system. Decentralized regions have disadvantages linked to their geographical position, but the inhabitants of these areas should reach relevant destinations with the same travel speed as the people in the central regions.

The TEN-T's actual effects on accessibility are still unknown, because some projects can increase the accessibility of some regions, but they do not improve the accessibility of other neighbouring regions. Anyway, a more integrated land network could be a successful element to increase the accessibility to airports, mainly regional airports, thus starting the development of such airports and a more effective distribution of demand over the EU territory.

Anyway, the land transport infrastructure facilities required for airports depend on how the airport network develops and then which is the more suitable European integrated network. Development of airports in turn depends on the development of the airline market and the policies adopted by local and national governments.

2.4 Air-rail competition/integration

As addressed by the EC, air and rail transport systems should become more complementary. Actually, there is a need for efficient co-modal infrastructures and modal split for airport access should also be improved. The EC exhibits particular attention towards projects concerning inter-modal infrastructures that are encouraged by means of the European Cohesion Policy and continue to be eligible for financing under the European Regional Development and Cohesion Funds, still available for the period 2007–2013. The Commission also invites Member States to support the development of inter-modal inter-changes at airports (rail links to and railway stations at airports), which promote efficiency of both rail and air transport.

Anyway, the point of view in most adopted policies (both at national and over-national levels) is to establish competing high-speed rail services to meet at least some of the current and future demands on some links, in order to substitute air services with rail services.

At least three interfaces between air and rail exist that can produce positive impacts on the environment:

- links to the city, that can produce decongestion of road traffic and better air quality around airports;
- links to the region, that can have the same benefits as above and the additional benefit of the airport catchment area expansion;

- link between the airport and major metropolitan areas by means of high-speed rail with the same benefits as above and additional potential for short haul slots to be freed for long-haul flights, which for airports and air carriers represent higher slot productivity.

At the moment, the railway European network can be classified as conventional rail and high-speed rail (Figure 3).

Figure 3: The European main railway network (2008).

Conventional rail can play an important role to connect secondary and regional airports; where such links lack, they should be planned by Member States and Community funding can also be done to realize these infrastructures.

As defined in the European Directive on Interoperability, high-speed rail is a system where trains run at a maximum speed of at least 250 kilometres/hour. The boundary between high-speed and conventional rail can also be unclear, as some conventional trains in the UK and Sweden achieve better average speeds than, for example, high-speed trains in Germany even though the latter achieve better maximum speeds.

The opening of high-speed lines, such as Paris-Lyon and Madrid-Seville, has enabled rail transport to obtain significant market shares on routes where time-sensitive passengers would previously have travelled by air. Anyway, due to the air liberalization process, the expansion of low-cost airlines has produced on some routes, particularly in Germany and the UK, prices for air transport similar to or below rail transport fares that could reverse the switch in market share. In addition, the construction and maintenance of high-speed rail lines require significant public funding. But the role of high-speed lines is more complex, because they can act not only as competitors against air transport, but also as complementary mode to increase the catchment area of an airport, mainly hub or primary airports. Then, conventional rail can increase the connections between secondary and regional airports enabling them to split air traffic according to their policies; on the other hand, high-speed rail can be seen as a key factor to obtain significant decrease in air congestion, as they can replace air links on some routes. Finally, they can increase the accessibility at the main airports and provide additional demand from a larger catchment area mainly for long-haul trips, as for short trips high-speed trains can replace the air mode. As an example, two European airports, Frankfurt and Paris CDG, have high-speed rail stations at the airport and there is the potential for rail and air services to complement each other rather than compete. Instead of taking a short distance flight to the airport, in order to connect on a longer distance flight, passengers can travel by high-speed rail to/from the airport. As integrated transport system network should also provide fare integration, on some routes passengers can buy tickets which include both a rail sector and the air sector. However, the attractiveness of such an integrated system to air passengers is limited if they cannot check-in their luggage at the station and obtain a single electronic ticket for the combined journey, due to the severe measures undertaken by the EC in terms of security. On the other hand, the absence of integrated air–rail tickets can be seen as an obstacle to the further development of air/rail inter-modality in terms of services and passenger interest.

Finally, air/rail inter-modality cannot be considered as a primary way to decongest airports as the decongesting effect amounts to 1 or 2 years of air traffic growth. However, it is useful to achieve a greater efficiency of the transport system and in particular of airports where the environmental burden will be reduced.

To encourage rail as a complement for air, attention should be given on improving the attraction on the rail product for both point-to-point and transfer journeys.

The principal drivers for passengers when choosing a mode of transport are relatively stable and consistently important across Europe. As investigations on passenger behaviour show, users will choose a transport mode among a set of available modes that match their trip exigencies when time, fare, frequency, access and also information, ticketing, languages, service integration and other issues, offer them an advantage with respect to the alternative modes. Then, users will choose the rail option with respect to air if its characteristics are overall better. Inter-modal development should therefore understand the passenger market choices.

The main factors determining air and rail market share can be identified in the following:

- the operating costs of each mode;
- the expected trend in market share and operating costs in the next 5–10 years;
- the security aspects concerned with the introduction of through baggage handling and e-ticketing;

- reliability;
- terminal accessibility.

For the last two points, as an example, the excellent reliability of the high-speed trains in Spain was a key factor determining the high market share of the Madrid–Seville rail service. Similarly, the good location of the airports on the Madrid–Barcelona route contributed to high air market share; in contrast, the relatively poor location of the airports on the Paris–Marseille route contributed to high rail market share.

The choices of passengers between air and rail are then driven by the combination of the relevant attributes as times and costs, where times include trip time, waiting time at terminals, access/egress times and so on. In terms of costs (as air/rail fares, parking or bus tickets to reach the terminal and so on) the belief here is that rail is generally less costly than air. This is true in principle, mainly if the comparison is between conventional trains and full-service (or traditional) air carriers, while the difference is much less significant (and in some cases it is reversed) if the comparison is between high-speed rail services and low-cost air carriers.

For example, for the London–Paris and London–Edinburgh routes, the rail mode is on average the cheapest option (Steer Davies Gleave Report [8]). However, while rail fares on the London–Paris route were nearly as high as those of the main traditional operators, on the London–Edinburgh route, low-cost air carriers offer on average better fares than the rail operator. This could be the main reason for the low rail market share on this route, as airlines on the London–Edinburgh link offer relatively lower fares.

As investments in multimodal interchange nodes and the connecting road and rail links have a long time-horizon, then the actual potential for competitiveness vs. integration should be carefully evaluated.

To conclude this section, another important project that can further increase the land accessibility among neighbouring nations within the EU is the innovative European Rail Traffic Management System (ERTMS) that introduces digital technology for the European rail infrastructure. As for the air transport, there are different signalling systems in the cab of the train for the various national networks, but ERTMS standard train protection system will greatly simplify and speed up the technical interoperability of cross-border transports. Further advantages will be the increase in safety standards to a high common level throughout the EU as well as the increase in the capacity utilization of the existing rail network (ERTMS [9]).

3 Airports in the EU perspective

The role of airports in Europe is a matter of discussion, mainly because of their double nature: as important node of air network (but also as node of inter-modal networks) and as source of employment and potential economic engine for a region.

Solutions to increase airport safety, capacity and efficiency while remaining environmentally friendly are the main goals of the EUROCONTROL Airport

Operations Programme (APR), first launched in January 2002 and then, due to its success, in January 2007.

As recent data provide, in 2006 in Europe there were about 2100 airports, with a great part being regional and secondary airports. They are spread on the territory, so potential passengers can reach them on average in 90 minutes. The cities closest to European busiest airports have between 4 and 46 airfields within 100 kilometres from the city centre.

The largest European airports get 80% or more of all departures within 100 kilometres (EUROCONTROL [10]), the usual distance of these airports from the city centres being about 20–25 kilometres. In terms of distribution on the territory, large cities are far from large airports no more than 50–150 kilometres in Northern Europe, while in Southern Europe the separation among the main cities, and then large airports, is larger. As an example, the main airport serving Madrid is 13 km from the city centre, but the next airport with more than 100 departures/day is 290 kilometres away, at Valencia.

In terms of ownership, many airport types can be identified, due to different historical and political perspectives in the EU Member States and the Accession countries. Several ownership categories can be recognized, but there are also mixed ownership (public/private) whose difference is in the proportion of national and local government involvement. To give an overview, the airport ownership types can be identified in the following:

- national government;
- regional/local government owned;
- other state sector ownership;
- chamber of Commerce;
- privatized airport/airport group;
- mixed type: majority government ownership;
- mixed type: minority government ownership.

Within the different airport categories, regional airports are a potential challenge for the European air network. In fact, they can provide additional capacity in areas where major airports have become congested, but given their inherent small nature they may not be making sufficient revenue to cover their costs.

These two points are discussed in the following.

Regional airports have become progressively more important in the European aviation network as air demand has increased and many new airlines, particularly low-cost air carriers, have begun to operate at small airports. Then, from one hand regional airports have increased access to aviation markets for a larger proportion of the population that otherwise could not use the air mode. On the other hand, they have increased competition among airlines because of their attractive potential for many air carriers, thus leading to lower fares, increased frequencies and more served destinations. More factors can be identified as crucial for the progressive development of regional airports, as the growth and expansion of the number of regional carriers, the rise of the low-cost carrier, the conversion of military airfields into commercial service airports and the increased use of larger regional jets.

Anyway, the liberalization process has produced remarkable changes not only in the airline industry but also in the airport industry, although most of them have maintained their profitability from both location and, in some cases, monopoly rents. For regional airports, however, the question is more complex. Although the number of movements in such airports has increased significantly as well as the number of passengers and/or goods, however the absolute numbers are quite low and then they may have insufficient revenue to cover their costs.

According to the airport European data, there is significant variation across both cost and revenue performances. Some airports have high costs but also high operating revenues. Efficient airports can be considered those providing economically efficient levels of output; anyway, for airports the output is a combination of aircraft movements and handled passengers, so different airport rankings are obtained when comparing cost per passenger vs. cost per movement.

Another aspect concerns the potential competition among airports and then which is their effective role with respect to the air services generally they offer. As nodes of the air network, airports provide links between locations at given times and costs (also due to the airline offer) and they compete for passengers by competing for airlines and airline services. The passenger airport choices are based on the combination of airport and airline characteristics (see also Chapter 5). Airlines, in turn, will choose the airport where to start the service on the basis of many factors including network fitness and airline business model.

Regional airports will compete on comparable full price over their catchment area in order to attract a level of demand able to increase the revenue, both due to aviation and non-aviation services and, as some analyses show, there is an increasing level of competition between regional and secondary airports as well as between the secondary airports themselves.

To start a convenient process of airport competition, there should be effective available alternative airports and the willingness of airlines to compete with the air services offered at the current dominant airports. But also passengers should be willing to move from the dominant airport to the potential competitive one, on the basis of the air services they can obtain at the latter. Airport competition has the potential to expand further if factors such as attractiveness of the low-fare airlines and of the airports they serve combine together to become appealing for passengers.

The main attractive factors for airlines are:

- the reduced airport turnaround times (e.g. 25–30 minutes on average) that enable airlines to increase the productivity of planes and their crews when compared to the slot-constrained hub airports;
- the lower airport charges they can obtain at secondary and regional airports.

Other factors that encourage airlines to introduce air services for new city-pair markets are:

- potential traffic and yield at each end of route;
- availability of slots;

- existing competition offered by other airlines on route and indirect routings;
- operating costs not dependent on airport operators.

Attractive factors for passengers to move towards a new airport are not only reduced air fares (generally offered at secondary or regional airports), but also reduced delays (as these airports do not suffer from traffic congestion) and direct point-to-point services (that avoid waiting time for transfers at an intermediate hub airports). Finally, when a delay occurs at smaller airports it is generally worse than at larger airports, but delays at smaller airports are relatively infrequent (actually most of the total delay takes place at large airports) and this may represent a compensation for the lower frequencies generally offered to passengers.

The choice of passengers to move towards an airport and airlines to start new services can be helped by the airport that can play an important role in stressing the attractions of the airport infrastructure and surrounding area for business and leisure travellers, but also can influence such decisions directly by offering good facilities (parking, surface access, check-in, lounges, shopping, gates, and sometimes handling services), and suitable cost of landings and take-offs.

When two or more airports share a similar catchment area, the airline decision to introduce the service at all and to use a given airport will strongly depend on the airport offer. Airports close to the same urban area are in the best position to compete with each other, given their proximity to the commercial and residential centres of the city; in this case, great relevance assumes the identification of their overlapping catchment area, where two or more airports (or, better, airlines operating at those airports) compete for the same air demand (see also Chapter 4).

In terms of connection and frequency, scheduled traffic at an airport grows by adding connections and by increasing frequency on a small proportion of those connections. Two kinds of offered air services can be identified as hub-an-spoke vs. point-to-point.

The hub-and-spoke system is used by many full-service air carriers as the preferred one in order to increase the load factor on average and to gain a monopolistic power at airports. A hub-and-spoke system is characterized by a high spatial network concentration, a time coordination of flights at the hub, according to a 'flight wave' concept, and the integration of the air services at the hub (as baggage transfer). The coordination at hubs means that delays in only one flight can have consequences on many other flights (e.g. crew or aircraft unavailability). An airport can play the role of 'hub' for a hub-and-spoke network if it is centrally located with respect to the served market and there is a significant demand starting/ending trips at hubs. Furthermore, it should guarantee suitable facilities to accommodate large aircraft and the baggage transfer, as well as all the accessory facilities required by airlines in doing a hub-and-spoke service.

Point-to-point services are simply routes serving a given city-pair where there is a significant demand to guarantee the accomplishment of the break-even load factor. In this case, passengers can fly from an origin airport to a destination one without scheduled transfers at intermediate airports and then without loss of accessories time (e.g. due to baggage recovery and waiting time). Generally, the used aircraft are smaller at the first time and larger if demand increases after the service has started; the flown distances are within 400 kilometres from medium-sized airports, while smaller airports can still have shorter flights.

There is a general agreement that the trend is towards smaller aircraft for intra-European services if market trends will continue. That could imply more point-to-point services and the growth in the use of smaller, regional airports. A point-to-point increase in passenger travel would require the extension and upgrading of smaller airports and a redesign of the network.

Anyway, the question is whether the changes in the market structure observed in the airline industry will be permanent, or they are simply transitory stages on the path towards a different, long-run equilibrium. Two opposite beliefs are proposed: some airport network planners state that the determinants of the hub-and-spoke system are not set to decrease in the near future and the current factors promoting the growth of point-to-point services may weaken in the next future; on the contrary, some others seem convinced that point-to-point services will predominate in the long run. This latter point of view is also encouraged by some studies carried out in the USA on the development of the US airport system that predict a huge increase of point-to-point links by 2020 with almost all passengers being offered direct flights to their destinations, an improvement in services and a reduction in the number of takeoffs and landings relative to the volume of transport services.

Some final considerations about the tendencies concerning the development of airports in Europe, and mainly regional airports, is the question of State aids, funding for transport links and regulation measures.

State aids are intended as local, regional or national government measures to assist airports (and airlines), and they may fall within Article 87(3)(a) of the EC Treaties if their location is within an eligible region, thus being particularly relevant for regional airports. EC *Guidelines on regional airport State aid* affirm that regional airport operators have to inform the Commission about any public finance they receive from regional or national authorities, as well as by means of the EU funds. Notified aid is then examined by the Commission and if there is doubt that certain investment at a regional airport constituted unauthorized State aid, the Commission can start a formal investigation against the concerned airport.

In the context of subsidies for airlines that realize a public service for some specified routes which they would not normally operate on economic basis, there are some specific indications. Such subsidies can be allowed in two cases:

• when other transport systems cannot guarantee a suitable accessibility to some regions, the local or central authority identify some scheduled air routes to serve airports located in peripheral areas or developing regions, or alternatively low-demand routes provided that such measures can be considered crucial for the economic development of a given geographical area (public service obligation, as defined in Council Regulation 2408/92,

currently under revision); such subsidy then serves to reimburse a carrier selected by a public tender for performing the required public service;
- where the subsidy has a social character granted to specific categories of passengers on a route granted without discrimination on the grounds of the carrier operating the services.

Another aspect considered in the Guidelines concerns an airline that can receive significant financial advantages by obtaining from the public authority, or the entity that operates the airport on behalf of the authority, exclusive concessions for a market price lower than their actual market value. Although the exclusive concession may be given to an airline for a price lower than its market value, if the airline pays no fee for the exclusivity or the fee is lower than would be paid under normal commercial conditions, that should be considered an aid element.

State aids to airports may have as consequence a distortion in competition, both among airports and airlines. In fact, direct or indirect subsidization of airports can distort competition between airports themselves, while subsidization of the airports could indirectly benefit airlines, thus distorting competition between them as the aid enables airports to facilitate specific airlines by means of, for example, lower airport charges.

Funding for transport links, in order to connect airports to the land transport systems, falls within the EC Guidelines on finance for infrastructure, open to all potential users without discrimination. As already discussed, these improved transport connections may extend an airport catchment area, thus improving its competitiveness; funds from the Community TEN-T can also be used by airports for improving inter-modal links following the wide Community transport policy. This kind of funding does not constitute State aid as the funds derive from the central EU funding, and then the construction of a high-speed rail link, rail-air station or a people-mover link to an airport terminal is unlikely to be considered a State aid.

Finally, regulation should be confined to those activities in which the airport has constant monopoly power, as airport services essential for downstream users that cannot be duplicated without considerable costs. The airside system, included aprons, and the passenger and freight handling terminals are generally regarded as such services. On the contrary, non-aviation activities and ground handling are seen as activities in which, at a given extent, the airport might have some monopolistic power. As the air liberalization process extends to several features, also ground handling was liberalized in 1996, thus enabling third party providers to enter the market. Ground handling services should not be regulated, but central infrastructure services such as package handling systems should be part of the regulated activities. In countries where airports do not offer ground handling (as in the UK) this does not represent a problem, but in the majority of the European Nations (as Italy, Spain, France, Austria, Germany) airports provide ground handling services and then the way towards the effective liberalization will be longer.

4 Low-cost carriers and regional airports

The European deregulation has generated a massive expansion in a segment of the airline industry known as 'no frills' or 'low-cost' airlines. There has been a significant entry of new airlines offering single-class services on a point-to-point basis. Low-cost air carriers have risen quickly in the last years, thus making the air transport system more accessible to many users, mainly to young and low-income people, but today also businessmen are attracted by the competitive fares proposed by low-cost air carriers. While the market share of these low-cost carriers was still relatively low in 2000/2001, the number of successful carriers increased noticeably.

In Europe, the growth of low-cost and regional carriers has led to a greater use of secondary and local airports with few or no international connections prior to deregulation. On the other hand, it can be argued that the expansion of the low-cost carrier is mainly linked to the available overcapacity at regional airports.

The low-cost models adopted by air carriers to reduce their operational costs in order to maintain a high competitiveness in terms of air fares, can be different among the different companies (Gillen and Lall [11]), but some common factors can be identified, also with respect to full-service air carriers, mainly in the commercial, organizational and technical fields.

In terms of commercial aspects, low-cost carriers achieve significant savings by selling their tickets via Internet or in same cases by means of payment call-centres. Furthermore, the ticket is just a reference code (sent by e-mail after the flight has been purchased) that has to be presented at the check-in point together with the passport in order to receive a boarding card, often without seat reservation. Finally, low-cost air carriers generally do not adopt fidelity programmes (as frequent flier programmes).

In terms of organizational aspects, low-cost air carriers have reduced all the services   not included in the transport function, as on-board meals, magazines and drinks that are not included in the fare and can be bought on the airplane during the flight. Cabin crew and ground staff are also reduced and many services considered unessential for the development of the company are outsourced. Furthermore, they offer medium distance flights, generally intra-EU for the European case: on average, flights cover about 800 kilometres. The service is organized on a point-to-point base, thus avoiding baggage and passenger transfers and maintaining a low turnaround time. In fact, smaller airports can offer only limited opportunities to transfer to other flights, while major airports may suffer from delays which can make connections unsure. Generally, frequencies are not high because low-cost air carriers frequently offer air services between low-demand, secondary airports, although, in many cases, with a great potentiality (as Hahn for Frankfurt, Beauvais for Paris, Charleroi for Brussels, Bergamo for Milan). In this light, secondary, or regional, airports have great advantages for low-cost air carriers and also for passengers in terms of reduced waiting time in the baggage claim area and walking time inside the terminal as well as less congestion inside the airport. The main disadvantages for passengers of regional airports are the higher access/egress times between the city-centre of their actual destination and the airport itself.

In terms of technical aspects, low-cost carriers have low turnaround time in order to use more efficiently their aircraft. As an example, turnaround times for low-cost carriers are about 25–35 minutes, while for full-service carriers they range from 45 to 60 minutes. Then, generally low-cost carriers can use their aircraft 30% more than full-service carriers thus realizing more flights per aircraft. Furthermore, for intra-EU flights the number of flown hours per aircraft is on average 9 per day for full-service carriers and about 10–12 for low-cost carriers. Finally, full-service carriers generally use a mixed fleet while low-cost carriers use a unique type of aircraft (generally B-737). This enables the air carriers to spend less for crew training and to have significant savings in terms of aircraft maintenance.

The first significant example of low-cost air carrier in Europe is Ryanair. At the beginning, Ryanair tried to offer the same air services as the full-services airlines it faced (as British Airways and Aer Lingus), but with lower fares in order to be more attractive for passengers.

However, the high operational costs produced a significant loss in the period 1985–1991 (apart from 1987) by convincing the airline managers to transform Ryanair in a cash driven airline with a reduction of the offered services and the adoption of strategies to limit costs of the kind usually identified as 'low-cost' models. Among the different measures, Ryanair outsourced all the passenger services considered unessential for the mission of the company. Outsourced services have advantages and disadvantages: from one hand, they enable the company to obtain a quick economic expansion by offering services to passengers without taking on staff working only on that specific aspect; on the other hand, the relationships with the subcontractors are time consuming and source of stress for the company, because a problem with one of the subcontractors can produce discomfort to passengers. After, Ryanair adopted and improved the low-cost/low-fare business model originally developed in the US by Southwest Airlines, by going progressively towards a business model based on single fleet type, use of uncongested airports, low turnaround times, point-to-point services and on-line bookings.

As Ryanair started its services between the UK and Ireland as direct concurrent of Aer Lingus (see, e.g. Figure 4) and then between the British Isles (from airports such as Stansted, Luton, Manchester, Newcastle, Glasgow and Dublin) and continental Europe, the impact of the low-cost segment was greatest in UK, where the number of passengers carried by Easyjet, a new low-cost entry following a similar low-fare approach, and Ryanair was 84% of the total British Airways passenger.

The rise of further low-cost airlines gave (and still is giving) a higher profile to European secondary airports and created new markets for air travel. For example, within Britain congestion at London airports encouraged the growth of many regional airports. Scotland Edinburgh Airport, for instance, increased significantly its traffic after being identified as a low-cost destination by some low-cost carriers.

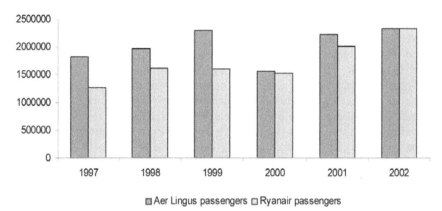

Figure 4: Aer Lingus and Ryanair passenger traffic on Ireland–London routes.

In contrast to Ryanair, EasyJet Airline has largely avoided secondary airports. Apart from Liverpool in northwest England and the airline home base at London Luton, EasyJet has concentrated on serving primary airports. Routes are guaranteed on major destinations as Barcelona, Nice, Paris, Zurich, Geneva and Amsterdam, and in the future of the company there could be a change towards higher fares as EasyJet managers expect that people will pay more to travel to main airports.

Nowadays, low-cost carriers are expanding services on continental Europe. Ryanair is developing Frankfurt-Hahn and Charleroi as bases while EasyJet is developing Geneva. The trend at the major airports has been towards a continued pressure for additional slots but in some cases there has been a contraction in the served destinations, perhaps because some airlines focused on their most profitable routes due to some current economic situations.

An important aspect that has promoted the use of regional airports is the opportunity for low-cost companies to obtain subsidies in the form of discounted airport charges. In fact, some regional airports have undertaken this way to stimulate traffic and then to increase the revenue. However, discounts offered to airlines by airport operators may be considered State aid if they discriminate against particular airlines. In some cases, the analysis of the circumstances by the EC have stated that 'discounted landing fees would not constitute State aid where they were applied for a limited duration and were available to all airlines operating from the airport, subject to their fulfilling objective criteria (i.e. starting a new service to a new destination)' (Manchester Airport case, EC). In other cases, agreements between airport operators and airlines or the independent application of a discriminatory policy by the airport operator have led to discounted airport charges and, therefore, Articles 81 and 82 of the EC Treaties, as opposed to Article 87, have been used to challenge discriminatory airport charges. Such situations distort competition for airports that cover their costs and may lead to inefficiencies for passengers and airlines. This was the key issue in the Charleroi Airport–Ryanair case, where, following the EC, aid was made available only to Ryanair. Anyway, a recent sentence of the European Court has reversed the EC judgment.

One of the most controversial questions about the great success of Ryanair in Europe mainly concerns the negotiation of the airport charges realized by the managerial staff of the airline. Many Ryanair competing air carriers have denounced the application of advantage fees to Ryanair by airport operators and have asked the EC for a clarification. Actually, data for eight provincial airports in UK indicate that Ryanair has negotiated airport charges with at least a two-thirds discount on the Stansted charge.

Finally, regional airport development has been often associated with passenger traffic. However, the growth in the air freight transport has led to a similar re-valuation of the role of regional airports as the emergence of passenger low-cost carriers. In fact, smaller airports, some of them being the former military airports with only basic service functions, now serve as specialized freight airports. Compared to primary and secondary airports with freight and passenger services and international connections, they are located further away from the larger cities, with far fewer connections to the supra-regional railway and road network. But the same measures (and the same considerations), as for regional airports used by passengers, can be adopted for these freight-specialized airports.

5 Conclusions

Many policies have been undertaken by the EU to promote the development of the transport system within Europe, following an integrated approach as stated by the TEN-T project.

Significant progresses have also been realized in the air transport system, also due to the urgency to achieve integration and harmonization among the different aviation procedures in the several European Nations.

The considerable congestion at the main airports and the liberalization process, enabling low-cost carriers to offer passengers lower-fare services, are the main factors underlying the current development of regional airports. Available capacity and demand potential have been key factors for the progressive growth of more regional airports, also helped by the EU general policy addressed to environment friendly transport strategies.

The significant growth of point-to-point flights offered by low-cost carriers is also associated with the use of smaller airports, often far from metropolitan centres or even metropolitan areas.

Low-cost airlines have also played a determinant role for the growth of both air traffic and regional airports. At least to some extent, their expansion has been made possible by overcapacity at regional airports. Furthermore, as there is little extra cost involved in giving low-cost carriers access to unused capacity available at airports, airport charges might also   be low.

The question that can be posed is whether this will be the tendency in Europe. In other words once spare capacity has been used up, airport costs in the regional airports might increase substantially. Then, additional capacity can be provided on the basis of the demand for airport services at fares which cover the full costs.

On the other hand, spare capacity is also due to competition among airports; airports with larger capacities can obtain economies of scale while potentially competing airports may outperform one another. Anyway, without a right planning of the airport system the risk is to produce overcapacities often due to the authorities themselves that try to stop the development of other potential competing airports in order to attract business and the associated tax revenues. Overcapacities, in turn, require government subsidies thus creating uneconomical cycles. A right planning policy and a great coordination among local authorities can avoid over-investment at regional airports, even if this could produce higher airport costs for the carriers using these airports but also lower public expenditure on subsidizing them. Investment decisions require either greater centralization or mechanisms for cooperation between local authorities which would otherwise be in competition.

In any case, as statistical data provide, the growth of regional airports, also supported by the EU policies, seems unavoidable by now, but the increasing importance of smaller airports (often decentralized with respect to the actual destination city) in the overall airport network could lead to a general worsening of the road transport intensity of the surface transport deriving from air travel.

Then, it is fundamental that the EU faces the problem of the right integration among all the different transport modes, in order to achieve the expected result: a multimodal connectivity in a really integrated transport network.

References

[1] Upham, P., Thomas, C., Gillingwater, D. & Raper, D., Environmental capacity and airport operations: Current issues and future prospects. *Journal of Air Transport Management*, **9**, pp. 145–151, 2003.

[2] Upham, P., Raper, D., Thomas, C., McLellan, M., Lever, M. & Lieuwen, A., Environmental capacity and European air transport: stakeholder opinion and implications for modelling. *Journal of Air Transport Management*, **10**, pp. 199–205, 2004.

[3] Regulation (EC) No 793/2004 of the European Parliament and of the Council of 21 April 2004 amending Council Regulation (EEC) No 95/93 on common rules for the allocation of slots at Community airports, Strasbourg, 21 April 2004.

[4] Postorino, M.N., Barrile, V. & Cotroneo, F., Surface movement ground control by means of a GPS–GIS system. *Journal of Air Traffic Management*, **12**, pp. 375–381, 2006.

[5] White Paper, European Transport policy for 2010: Time to decide, European Commission, September 2001.

[6] European Commission, Multi-annual indicative TEN-T programme (MAP) for the period 2007–2013, COM(2004)475, 14 July 2004.

[7] European Commission, Multi-annual indicative TEN-T programme (MAP) for the period 2007–2013, COM(2006)245, 25 May 2006.

[8] Steer Davies Gleave, Air and Rail competition and complementarity, Final Report prepared for the European Commission DG TREN, 2006.

[9] European Rail Traffic Management System (ERTMS), http://ec.europa.eu/transport/rail/interoperability/.

[10] EUROCONTROL, A place to stand: Airports in the European air network. *Trends in Air Traffic*, Vol. 3, 2007.

[11] Gillen, D. & Lall, A., Competitive advantage of low-cost carriers: Some implications for airports. *Journal of Air Transport Management*, **10**, pp. 41–50, 2004.

3

The development of regional airports in Asia

Y-C. Chang
National Taiwan Ocean University, Taiwan

Abstract

Countries in Asia are more diverse politically, economically and culturally than those in North America and Europe, with each of them differing in their approach to deregulation. This chapter reviews and analyses the regional airports development in Asia. It concludes that Asian airport operators will be facing a challenging time ahead with air traffic growth at a reduced pace and volatility in fuel prices affecting airline business. In addition, the LCCs continuing growth in Asia, consumer need for point-to-point travel and scarcity of secondary airports in Asia have opened up many opportunities for airport operators and investors.

Keywords: Taiwan; China; ASEAN; low-cost carriers.

1 Introduction

1.1 Characteristics of Asian air transport industry

Over the past few decades, Asia has grown more rapidly than any other part of the world economy. Its trade and industrial transformation has been built upon openness and integration into the world economy, with a continual process of reform and liberalization in a succession of Asian economies. The strong economic growth led to a rapid increase in the demand for air travel in the region of Asia.

Total international scheduled passenger traffic to, from and within the region grew by 7.4% per annum on average between 1985 and 2005. The global share of Asia-Pacific international scheduled passenger traffic increased from 25.5% in 1985 to 28.3% in 2005. The airlines of Asia-Pacific region are expected to show the highest growth in passenger traffic, at 5.8 % per annum through to the year 2025, while the airlines of North America are anticipated to show the lowest growth, around 3.6% per annum. As a result of the projected growth in passenger traffic, the airlines of the Asia-Pacific region are expected to increase their share of world passenger traffic (in terms of passenger-kilometres) by about 6.5% points to 32.52%, the highest among all the regions, with their share of total international scheduled passenger traffic increasing to about 33.7% (see Figure 1, International Civil Aviation Organisation [11]).

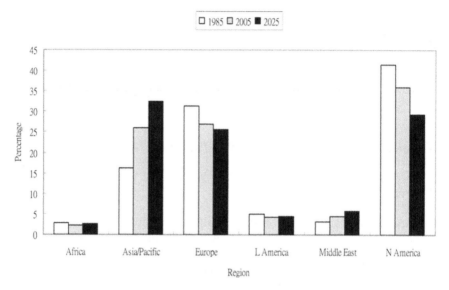

Figure 1: Share of total international scheduled passenger traffic by each region.

Table 1 reveals that regional platforms enjoyed the highest year-on-year growth on a percentage basis, up 7.3% against a 5.6% rise for Intercontinental hubs and 5.4% for Secondary hubs. Regional platforms in Asia/Oceania were still above the world average and well ahead of their counterparts in North America and Western Europe, owing mainly to the explosion of domestic traffic in China and India but also, and increasingly, in Indonesia and Vietnam (Air Transport World [4]).

Table 1: 2006–2007 Airport traffic growth by continental and airport type.

Airport type	World	Western Europe	North America	Unit: % Asia/Oceania
Intercontinental hubs	5.6	5.5	2.3	8.2
Secondary hubs	5.4	6.1	4.1	6.3
Regional platforms	7.3	6.7	4.2	10.7

Source: Air Transport World [4].

According to 'World Airport Traffic Analysis 2007' report, China and India continued to pull demand with a 70% share of the region's traffic volume increase in 2007 (Figure 2). China's airports handled some 395.4 million passengers, up 16.7%. It accounted for 54% of the region's growth or 17% of the world growth. Throughput at Indian airports rose 19.9% to 97.6 million whereas traffic in the region's second-largest market. Vietnam and Philippines recorded significant growth rates, up 25.8% and 20.4% respectively. The strong economic development, particularly in China and India, with an emerging middle and upper class has really stimulated air traffic demand. In addition, domestic markets are fuelling country and regional growth. Domestic traffic accounted for 54% of China's total growth in 2007 (Figure 3). In India, the imbalance between domestic and international travel was even more pronounced; domestic traffic accounted for 96% of the growth in passenger throughput in 2007. In Vietnam, 63% of the 3.9 million additional passengers in 2007 flew within the country whereas in Indonesia domestic travel soared 118%.

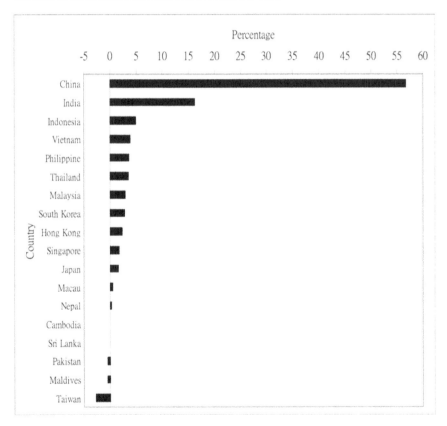

Figure 2:   Distribution of Asian airport traffic evolution by country 2007 *vs.* 2006. (passengers in millions)

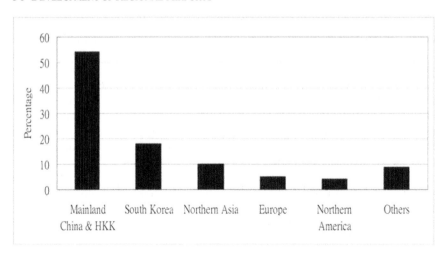

Figure 3: Split of mainland China growth per destination.

1.2 Trend of major international airport development

Given the rapid economic growth in Asia-Pacific, the region has a large number of busy airports, with twelve recording passenger traffic levels in excess of 20 million in 2007 (Table 2). Nine of the airports were ranked among the top 50 in the world in terms of passenger volume. In order to meet the growing demand and become regional hubs, substantial investment has been carried out in the region in recent years. New Kansai Airport opened in 1994, Hong Kong Chek Lap Kok Airport in 1998, New Kuala Lumpur Airport in 1999, Taipei CKS second terminal in 2000 and Seoul Incheon Airport in March 2001, Japan Nagoya Airport in 2005, second Bangkok International Airport in 2006, and Singapore Changi airport terminal 3 in 2008. In particular, Beijing's enormous Terminal Three opened in time for the Olympic Games in August 2008.

In these major international airports, Seoul Incheon Airport is the hub of Skyteam alliances in Asia; Singapore Changi and Bangkok Airports are the regional hubs for Star alliances; and Hong Kong Airport is the hub for Oneworld alliances.

1.3 Regional Airports in Asia

Due to the large number of airports in Asia, identifying the definition of regional airports becomes a difficult task. This chapter uses the Air Transport Intelligence Database [3] with the criteria, International Passengers less than one million, and Domestic Passengers more than 80 millions in 2007. The result comes out with 47 airports as showed in Table 3. Among these nations, Indonesia is the first country to liberalize its air transport sector. Indonesia is expected to have the fastest annual growth in international traffic during the 1990s, followed by Malaysia (Dempsey [10]). The government is planning to construct new airports at Medan and Padang in Sumatra, and in central Lombok.

Table 2: Major international airport characteristics in 2007.

Airport	Passenger(000)	Total Movements	Main hub airlines	Runways(metres)
Beijing Capital	53,737	399,697	Air China	1*3,800 1*3,200
Shanghai Pudong	28,930	187,045	China Eastern	1*3,300
Jakarta	31,987	248,482	Garuda Airlines	1*3,600 1*3,660
Tokyo Narita	35,530	195,074	Japan Airlines	1*4,000
Osaka Kansai	16,592	125,637	All Nippon Airways	1*3,500
Seoul Inchon	31,422	213,194	Korea Airlines Asiana Airlines	1*3,600 1*3,200
Kuala Lumpur	26,534	193,688	Malaysia Airlines [14]	1*4,000 1*4,019
Manila	20,468	188,797	Philippine Airlines	1*2,225 1*3,409
Singapore Changi	36,702	223,488	Singapore Airlines	1*4,000 1*3,260
Taipei CKS	23,426	160,120	China Airlines EVA Air	1*3,660 1*3,350
Bangkok	41,210	265,763	Thai Airways	1*3,700 1*3,500
Hong Kong	46,995	305,010	Cathay Pacific	2*3,800

Source: Air Transport Intelligence Database.

In these regional airports, some are popular tourist island airports, like Haikou in China, Bali in Indonesia, Jeju in Korea, Okinawa in Japan, Langkawi in Malaysia, and Phuket in Thailand. Because of their excellent weather and beautiful beach, these island airports attract lots of passengers each year. Bali is the most famous tourist island in Indonesia. Its Ngurah Rai – Bali International Airport started operation in 1931 by using a grass runway. The runway was upgraded during the period of 1941 to 1947 and lengthened to 1600 metres. It was named Tuban Airport as it's located in Tuban Village. Haikou Meilan International Airport is located on the southern island province of Hainan, which is partly-owned by the Hainan Airlines Group. It maintained a double-digits growth in passenger throughput, aircraft movements, and cargo throughput in 2008, and achieved the highest growth rate among the civil aviation airports in China. Phuket International Airport ranks second in Thailand in terms of passenger and cargo volume. Phuket Island and nearby provinces are popular resort areas and Phuket International Airport enjoys a large number of passengers from all over the world, and plays an important role in promoting travel and tourism in the southern region as well as throughout the kingdom. The airport is served by ten airlines, carrying more than 2.9 million passengers and

12,000 tons of cargo on 27,000 flights (data of 2007). The airport is located 32 km from downtown Phuket.

Table 3: Asia regional airport characteristics in 2007.

Country	Airport	Total passenger (in millions)	Total movements	Runways length*width (metres)
China	Haikou	7.265	63,416	Length: 11811
	Changsha	8.070	82,041	2600*45
	Dayong	1.517	14,148	2600*45
	Jinghong	1.808	17,506	2200*45
	Nanjing International	8.037	82,391	3600*45
	New Chitose	18.361	98,827	3000*60 3000*60
	Shanghai Hongqiao International	22.633	187,045	3300*58
	Shenzhen Baoan International	20.619	181,450	3400*45
	Xi'an Xianyang International	11.383	119,404	3000*45
India	Ahmedabad	3.038	39,280	3489*46
	Amritsar International	0.677	7,463	3289*45
	Gauahati	1.334	29,183	n.a.
	Goa	2.528	22,817	3430*46
	Jaipur	1.263	24,434	n.a.
	Nagpur	0.839	15,880	3164*46 1573*46
Indonesia	Ngurah Rai-Bali International	5.888	62,689	3000*45
	Banda Aceh	0.550	7,231	n.a.
	Bandung-Husein Sastranegara	0.361	6,397	n.a.
	Medan	5.004	53,795	2625*45
	Padang	1.753	14,995	n.a.
	Palembang	1.660	17,059	n.a.
	Pekanbaru	1.839	22,818	n.a.
	Pontianak-Supadio	1.379	17,898	n.a.
	Surabaya-Juanda	3.488	87,587	3000*45
	Ujung Pandang-Hasanuddin	1.600	51,698	n.a.
Japan	Tokyo Haneda	66.823	331,818	2500*45 3000*60 3000*60
	Fukuoka International	17.903	71,456	2800*60
	Kagoshima	5.591	n.a.	3000*45
	Okinawa Naha	14.951	123,596	3000*45

Table 3: Asia regional airport characteristics in 2007 (continued).

Country	Airport	Total passenger (in millions)	Total movements	Runways length*width (metres)
Korea	Jeju International	12.297	93,285	Length: 3000 Length: 1910
Malaysia	Penang	3.174	39,265	3352*45
	Bintulu	0.381	7,093	n.a.
	Kota Kinabalu International	4.537	52,047	Length: 2987
	Kuching	3.236	37,348	n.a.
	Kunming Wujiaba	15.729	148,185	3800*45
	Langkawi	1.123	10,828	3810*45
	Senai Airport	1.325	38,509	3800*46
	Subang - Sultan Abdul Aziz Shah	0.090	44,302	3780*45
Macau	Macau International	5.499	53,386	3360*45
Philippines	Diosdado Macapagal International	n.a.	n.a.	3200*45 3200*60
Taiwan	Kaoshiung International	5.717	67,149	2600*45 2700*60
Thailand	Phuket International	5.704	41,719	3000*45
	Bangkok Don Muang International	4.805	87,064	3700*60 3500*45
	Chiang Mai International	3.291	32,758	3100*45
	Chiang Rai International	0.754	7,743	3000*45
	Hat Yai International	1.390	16,687	3050*45
Vietnam	Hanoi Noi Bai International	6.371	44,353	Length: 3200 Length: 3800

Sources: Air transport intelligence database.

2 Aviation Policy

2.1 Different approach to deregulation

Although Asia has been the fastest growing air travel market in the world during the last two decades, air transport deregulation and liberalization in the region has been slower than in North America and Europe. Countries in Asia are more diverse politically, economically, and culturally than those in North America and Europe, with each of them differing in their approach to deregulation. Some countries, with strong economies and successful, well-established national airlines, developed countries with small populations, and countries that are isolated, have been strong advocates of liberalization, while others have been fearful of the consequences.

Singapore, the country with the smallest populations in this region, is keen to pursue more liberalized Air Services Agreements. Some countries have allowed a second national carrier to fly international routes in order to meet the rapidly rising demand and provide a better service. This has been the case in several countries, such as Hong Kong, Indonesia, Korea, Philippines, Taiwan, and Thailand. As the pressure for deregulation continues, China Civil Aviation Authority has restructured its domestic market. It merges its carriers into three groups, Air China, China Eastern, and China Southern, in order to strengthen its national airlines.

In Japan, the national government announced its Asia Gateway Plan, intended to liberalize Japanese skies, cut ticket prices and stimulate trade. Japan said Asia Gateway is the most radical liberalization of the highly regulated Japanese skies in decades. Tokyo wanted to open access for foreign carriers at regional airports, expand operations at Haneda airport and reduce limits on carriers flying from it. The country's aviation officials hope the policy will spur an Open Skies agreement with the Association of South East Asian Nations (ASEAN).

2.2 Aviation deregulation in Southeast Asia

The aviation deregulations in Southeast Asian countries are still progressing. Similar to EU, the trade circle within Southeast Asia is becoming smaller. To promote economic cooperation among Southeast Asian countries, ASEAN was established in 1976. The founding members were Malaysia, Thailand, Singapore, Indonesia, and the Philippines; Brunei (1984), Vietnam (1995), Burma (1997), Laos (1997), and Cambodia (1999) followed. Figure 4 is the map of ASEAN countries. The ASEAN region has population of around 500 million, total area of 4.5 million square kilometres, combined gross domestic product of almost US$700 billion, and total trade of about US$850 billion (About ASEAN [5]). The European Union (EU) established the first deregulation open skies policy in the world. The same question of open skies in Southeast Asia has been a topic of discussion at past ASEAN summits.

According to ASEAN's air transport deregulation policy, the ASEAN summit plans to open skies from capital city to capital city in 2008. In 2010, the member countries will open skies of a 'capital city + 1', which means, besides capital cities, each member country will open an airline in one additional city. From that point on up to 2015, the member countries will achieve 100% open skies in the ASEAN region. It proposes the formation of the ASEAN Airline Association to organize privately-owned airlines and provide greater accessibility. One of the largest disadvantages is the degree of deregulation in ASEAN countries that are not unanimous, nevertheless (Patel [18]). Singapore, Thailand, and Brunei joined the open skies pact in December 2004, and Indonesia government has already declared open skies to ASEAN in October 2006.

Figure 4: Map of Southeast Asia.

Once the air transport is deregulated, the low-cost carriers (LCCs) can compete to occupy the market without any restrictions. Furthermore, passengers are often faithful to the airline company that emerges first. In an attempt to take the leadership role in the air transport market, some of the main LCCs, such as AirAsia [1] and Jetstar [12], have implored to their governments to open skies to all ASEAN members. Hopefully, the ASEAN era of open skies will soon come.

2.3   Capital city airports reform

After some new hub airports operated in Asia, the old city airport was transferred into regional function, including Japan Tokyo Haneda Airport, Korean Seoul Gimpo Airport, Taiwan Taipei Shengshan Airport, Thailand Bangkok Don Muang Airport, and China Shanghai Hongqiao Airport.

2.3.1   Japan Tokyo Haneda Airport
Tokyo Haneda Airport is easily Asia's busiest airport, but it mainly handles domestic flights, with only limited international charters during overnight hours plus special shuttle flights during the day to Seoul's primarily domestic Gimpo airport and Shanghai's primarily domestic Hongqiao airport. The overnight charters began in 2001, while Gimpo flights began in 2003, followed by Hongqiao flights in 2007. Most of the international flights serving Tokyo operate to Narita airport, which is much further away from the Japanese capital's main

business districts. Business travellers in particular prefer Haneda and airlines have been looking forward to the opening of the long-awaited fourth runway in 2010. Congested Narita will in 2010 also have many new slots after an extension is completed of its secondary runway. Narita has an overnight curfew while 24-hour operations are allowed at Haneda (Airline Business [2]).

Until 2007, international charter flights were only allowed at Haneda between 23:00 and 06:00 but departures are now allowed from 20:30 and arrivals until 08:30. Ahead of the wider opening of Haneda to international flights, All Nippon Airways and Japan Airlines have been adding charter flights to key business destinations such as Hong Kong. Cathay Pacific Airways has also launched charter flights between Hong Kong and Haneda and says it hopes to eventually serve Haneda with scheduled flights.

2.3.2 Korea Seoul Gimpo Airport

Gimpo International Airport, commonly known as Gimpo Airport (formerly Kimpo International Airport) was the main international airport for Seoul and South Korea before it was replaced by Incheon International Airport in 2001. It is now the second largest airport in Korea.

Gimpo airport is located in the west of Seoul, Republic of Korea. It became primarily a domestic airport but it also handles limited international traffic from Tokyo's primarily domestic Haneda airport and Shanghai's primarily domestic Hongqiao airport. The services are popular with business travellers as Gimpo is closer to the centre of Seoul than Inchon. Nowadays Gimpo is giving new pleasures to airport travellers of enjoying the complex space, called 'Sky City' which is, a place of culture, leisure, and shopping.

2.3.3 Taiwan Taipei Songshan Airport

Taipei Songshan Airport, nucleus of Taiwan civil aviation, is located in the Songshan District of Taipei. It is easily accessible from the town centers. Total space of this airport is 182 hectare (civil aviation area: 83 hectares). The east-west runway can accommodate B-747 and smaller aircrafts. Several auxiliary facilities including navigation guide and aid equipment, and approach lights are installed, to facilitate low visibility and night landing. Eight air bridges are available for passenger boarding and deplaning. This airport operates on 24-hour basis with the exception of the 2300–0600 hour during which only limited control flights and engine test are allowed.

Situated in Metropolitan Taipei, the Taipei Songshan Airport is the hub of domestic air transport. As a result of the economic slowdown, the aviation market has become depressed. Consequently, the number of passengers has dropped by close to 10% in recent years. In the future, this Airport will offer flights to Japan, Korea, China, and other regional destination.

2.3.4 Thailand Bangkok Don Muang Airport

Don Muang Airport used to be Bangkok's main international airport. The situation changed when Bangkok's Suvarnabhumi airport opened in September 2006, the new airport became the international gateway and Don Muang was left for point-to-point domestic services. In December 2007, Thailand's airport authority decided to re-open Don Muang airport to scheduled international flights in an effort to relieve congestion at Suvarnabhumi airport and also to make Don Muang more viable financially. The biggest domestic operators at Don Muang airport are Thai Airways International and LCCs Nok Air [15] and One-Two-Go [16].

2.3.5 China Shanghai Hongqiao Airport

Although Shanghai is not the capital city, it is a charming city full of energy, and is an important gateway in China and a bridge connecting the outer world. To satisfy the needs of the operation of 'One City, Two Airports', Shanghai Airport Authority was established officially in February, 1998 upon the approval of Shanghai Municipal People's Government as a result of an important reform on the management of Shanghai airports. From then on, both Hongqiao International Airport and Pudong International Airport are under the uniform management and operation of Shanghai Airport Authority. Hongqiao International Airport is located in the western suburbs of Shanghai, only 13 kilometres away from the city centre. Currently, Hongqiao Airport mainly accommodates domestic flights and remains the backup function for international flights and regional flights.

Besides developing international flights, a Shanghai Hawker Pacific Business Aviation Centre has been established at Shanghai Hongqiao airport. This Aviation Centre is 49% owned by Australia's Hawker Pacific and 51% owned by the Shanghai Airport Authority. It will have a maintenance, repair, and overhaul operation due to be completed in August 2009. The MRO will handle heavy maintenance for aircraft including Dassault Falcons and Hawker Beechcraft types. The company is seeking to expand its offering to include Bombardier, Embraer and Gulfstream business jets, the hangar will accommodate a Boeing 737–800, a Gulfstream and another smaller aircraft simultaneously. The new business aviation centre at Shanghai Hongqiao will be significant, because the airport authority plans to transfer business jet operations from Shanghai Pudong to the new centre at Shanghai Hongqiao. Due to its proximity to the city centre Hongqiao should prove to be a popular choice among business travellers.

3 Air transport development between China and Taiwan

3.1 Traffic between Taiwan and China

Over the past two decades, demand for air transport between Taiwan and China has grown rapidly, partly in response to the economic development of the two countries, and also as a result of political factors. Passengers who travel between the two places always transit via Hong Kong or Macau. Although Taipei and Fuzhou are only 184 kilometres apart, air travel between these two cities is only possible via Hong Kong or Macau. The journey takes 4 hours and 50 minutes, and costs US$374, excluding airport taxes. The high travel cost owing to transit, along with the inconvenience of transferring flights and the additional flying time, has become a major annoyance to most travellers.

As an alternative to frequent flying customers, the Taiwan-Hong Kong route is one of the busiest routes in the world. The fly time between Taiwan to Hong Kong is only 110 minutes. In addition, there are about forty-one-way flights operated by five airlines for this route per day. Direct cross-strait flights, currently in a high-demand market, have been approved in July 2008. The distance between Taiwan and China is similar to that between the UK and the European mainland. The successful experiences of LCCs in Europe could be replicated in Taiwan and China (Figure 5) in the near future. The operational strategies of LCCs in Europe could present a model for Taiwanese and Chinese carriers.

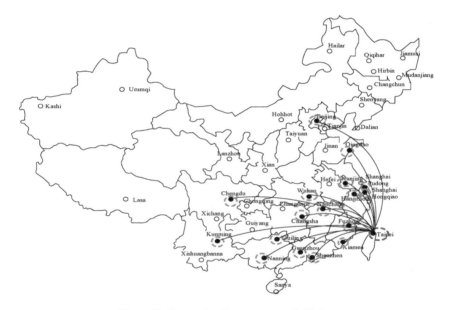

Figure 5: Routes for direct cross-strait flights.

3.2   Airports in China

Civil airports in China have been expanding rapidly since the 1990s. There were 142 airports operating in the country at the end of 2005, compared to 121 in 2000 and 109 in 1994. Twenty-five of these could facilitate aircraft of Boeing 747 size, and 113 could facilitate aircraft of Boeing 737 size (Table 4). China will have invested RMB 140 billion in airport construction in the 11th Five-Year Plan period which ends in 2010. By then it will have 186 airports, including three large-composite hubs, seven large regional hubs, 52 medium-size airports and 124 regional airports.

China has undertaken a massive civil aviation infrastructure effort to build new airports and expanded existing facilities. China's Xiamen Airlines is establishing a hub in Hunan province's Changsha city in co-operation with the Hunan provincial government. Within the next 12 months from April 2008 the airline will have three aircraft stationed at Changsha's Huanghua airport.

In May 2008, UPS announced the planned relocation of its Intra-Asia hub to Shenzhen from Clark Airport in the Philippines. The development is expected to cost US$180 million and become operational in 2010. The new hub is expected to cover an area of around 89,000 square metres and will include an express customs handling unit, sorting facilities (which will be 5 times the size of the Clark facility), cargo handling and ramp handling operations The relocation is expected to reduce shipment times for Asian customers by 1 day or more.

Table 4: Classification of Mainland China civil airports.

Flight area grade	Aircraft model	Number of years	Airport name
4E	B747	25	Beijing Capital, Shenyang Taoxian, Dalian Zhoushuizi, Harbin Taiping, Shanghai Hongqiao, Shanghai Pudong, Nanjing Lukou, Hanzhou Xiaoshan, Fuzhou Changle, Jinan Yaoqiao, Xiamen Gaoqi, Zhengzhou Zhengxin, Wuhan Tianhe, Guangzhou Baiyun, Shenzhen Baoan, Zhuhai Sanzao, Haikou Melan, Sanya Fenghuang, Chongqin Jiangbei, Chengdu Shuangliu, Kunming Wujiaba, Lhasa Gongga, Xi'an Xianyang, Urumchi Diguobao, Keshen
4D	B767 B757 MD82	35	Tianjin Binhai, Shijiazhuang Zhengding, Taiyuan Wushu, Huhehot Baita, Changchun Dafangshen, Changzhou Benniu, Lianyungang Baitafu, Xuzhou Guanyin, Ninnbo Lishe, Wenzhou Yongqiang, Chuanzhou Jinjiang, Zhoushan Zhujiajian, Hefei Luogang, Nanchang Changbei, Yantai Laishan, Qiangdao Liuting, Weihai Dashuibo, Weifang, Luoyang Beijiao, Yichang Sanxia, Changsha Huanghua, Zhangjiajie Hehua, Shantou Waisha, Naning Wuxu, Geermu, Liuzhou Bailian, Guilin Liangjiang, Xichang Qingshan, Kweyang Longdongbao, Changdu Bangda, Lanzhou Zhongchuan, Xining Caojiabao, Yinchuan Hedong, Hetian, Mianyang Nanjiao

Table 4: Classification of Mainland China civil airports. (continued)

Flight area grade	Aircraft model	Number of years	Airport name
4C	B737	53	Qinwangdao Shanhaiguan, Hailaer Dongshan, Baotou, Dandong Langtou, Jinzhou, Yanji Zhaoyangchuan, Qiqihar Sanjiazi, Jiamusi Dongjiao, Mudanjiang Hailang, Heihe, Nantong Xingdong, Yancheng, Huangyan Luqiao, Yidao, Quzhou, Huangshan Tunxi, Anqing, Fuyang, Wuyishan, Ganzhou Huangjin, Jingdezhen, Linyi, Dongying, Jiujiang Lushan, Nanyang Jiangying, Changde Taohuayuan, Zhanjiang, Yongzhou Lingling, Beihai Fucheng, Yilan Caibai, Jinyang, Guangyuan Panlong, Jiuzhai Huanglong, Panzhihua, Luzhou Lantian, Wanzhou Wuqiao, Zhaotong, Lijiang, Dali, Diqing, Simao, Baoshan, Tongren, Yanan, Dunhuang, Linchang, Wuzhou Changzhoudao, Wuxi Shuofang, Liancheng Guangmaoshan, Jinggangshan, Xiangfan Liuji, Liping, Anshun Huangguoshu
3C	Below B737	29	Xilin Haote, Tongliao, Wulan Haote, Wuhai, Chifeng, Manzhou Lixijiao, Changzhi Wangcun, Liancheng Zhangxiao, Datong Beijiazao, Chaoyang, Meixian, Enshi Xujiaping, Huaihua Zhijiang, Nanchong Gaoping, Xishuangbanna Gasa, Dehong Mangshi, Yulin Xisha, Hanzhong, Jiayuguan, Qingyang, Ankang, Yining, Aleitai, Akesu, Tacheng, Kuche, Kangerlei, Qiemo, Xingyi

Source: China Civil Aviation Authority, 2006. Analyses of Air Transport from Statistics, 2005, Beijing, China.

Zhuhai Airport, once China's largest white elephant airport, has made remarkable progress since Airport Authority Hong Kong entered into a joint venture management deal with the Zhuhai Municipal People's Government. Meanwhile, another Mainland airport, Hangzhou Xiaoshan International Airport, which is 35% owned by Airport Authority Hong Kong, plans to raise US$800 million from an initial public offering (IPO) by the end of the third quarter of this year, 2009. The Airport Authority's share will be reduced to 25% after the IPO.

3.3 Direct flights between Taiwan and China

On 4 July 2008, regular non-stop passenger flights between China and Taiwan have begun, nearly 60 years after the two sides split following a civil war. Six Chinese airlines and five Taiwanese airlines will be operating regularly between the two sides, with flights permitted from Friday through Monday each week.

Under the agreement, airlines from each side are allowed to operate 18 round-trip flights between Fridays and Mondays, between five Chinese cities and eight Taiwanese ports. In November 2008, an expanded deal was agreed to allow for a combined total of 108 weekly flights, which can be operated any day of the week. The expanded agreement also allows for a total of 60 cargo flights per week and increases to 21 from five the number of Chinese cities that can be served. Flights are allowed to seven Taiwanese airports, namely Taoyuan International Airport, Taichung International Airport, Taipei Shangshon International Airport, Kaoshiung International Airport, Mukun Airport, Hualien Airport and Taidong Airport. In China, 21 airports are allowed to fly to Taiwan, including Shanghai Pudong, Beijing Capital, Guangzhou Baiyun, Xiamen Gaoqi, Nanjing Lukou, Chengdu Shuangliu, Chongqin Jiangbei, Hanzhou Xiaoshan, Dalian Zhoushuizi, Guilin Liangjiang, Shenzhen Baoan, Wuhan Tianhe, Fuzhou Changle, Qiangdao Liuting, Changsha Huanghua, Haikou Melan, Kunming Wujiaba, Xi'an Xianyang, Shenyang Taoxian, Tianjin Binhai, and Zhengzhou Zhengxin. It is expected that the traffic will grow strongly in these airports in future in large part because of the new tourist demand.

3.4 Airport policy in China

Since all airports were transferred from the General Administration of Civil Aviation of China (CAAC) to provincial governments in mid-2004, with the exception of Beijing Capital International Airport and Lhasa Airport, China's civil airports have entered a new era. After the airport decentralization, each provincial government established a 100% state-owned airport management group company responsible for all civil airports inside the province. However, most of China's airports are losing money because there are not sufficient aircraft movements and local governments would find it very difficult to justify supporting the loss-making airports. So, the provinces look to 'big brothers' to help and advise them in the running of heir airports. The idea is that in the long-term the new system will be experienced enough to sustain itself.

Capital Airports Holding Company (CAH), Xiamen International Airport (Group) Co. Ltd, and Shanxi Airport Management Group are major airport groups. CAH, established in December 2002, now has a portfolio of 25 airports, which belong to airport management groups in Hubei, Guizhou, Jiangxi, Jilin, and Liaoning provinces and Beijing, Tianjin, and Chongqing municipalities, which are under the direct control of the central government. The market share of CAH's member airports was 30% in terms of passengers handled in 2005. Through asset restructuring, CAH now holds 65% of Beijing Capital International Airport Co. Ltd, which last year was the fastest growing of the world's top 30 hotels, according to Airports Council International (ACI). It handled 40.1 million passengers, up 17.5% year-on-year. Similarly, CAH also holds 100% in Tianjin and Chongqing airports and of Guizhou, Jiangxi, and Jilin Airport Management Groups. Through acquisition, CAH holds 100% of shares in Hubei and Liaoning Airport Management Groups (Orient Aviation [17]).

In addition, Xiamen International Airport Group Co. Ltd. manages three airports; Xiamen Gaoqi Airport, Fuzhou Changle Airport, and Longyan Airport, with total assets of about RMB 5 billion. The total passenger throughput in 2005 reached 10 million. Shanxi Airport Management Group consolidated with Ningxia and Qinghai groups in October 2004 and March 2006 respectively. They have a total of eight airports with Xian Xianyang Airport as the hub airport. It is anticipated that this move will accelerate airport growth as part of the West China development strategy. For many years, there have been three channels of airport financing in China. They are: the airport construction fees fund, started in 1992 and collected from passengers, financing by local government, and Chinese bank loans. Since the transfer to local governments, there have been more opportunities for airport financing such as commercial loans, domestic bonds, private sector investment, domestic cross-industry investments through airport corporatization and IPOs, foreign loans, international bonds, and investment or lease by foreign operators (Orient Aviation [17]).

In 2002, the CAAC, the former Ministry of Foreign Trade and Economic Cooperation and the State Development Planning Commission jointly issued 'Rules on Foreign Investment in the Civil Aviation Industry'. Foreign investors and airport operators expressed interest. For example, Copenhagen Airport acquired 20% of the Haikuo Meilan International Airport Company in 2002 and signed a 10-year consulting services contract which covered areas of capacity utilization and expansion, airport operations and the development of commercial activities. Haikuo Meilan is a listed company. In 2005, the airport handled seven million passengers and is ranked tenth in China. Copenhagen received a dividend of two million Danish krones (US$342,500) in 2004. Meilan Airport, meanwhile, earned 151.4 million yuan in 2005. In 2001, Aeroports de Paris acquired a 9.9% share in the Beijing Capital International Airport Co. Ltd. Last year Beijing Airport recorded a net profit of 915.5 million yuan, an increase of 20% over 2004. In June 2005, German airport operator, Fraport A.G., agreed to take a 25% stake in Ningbo International airport. In the same month, Singapore Changi International Airport signed an initial agreement to spend up to 1.6 billion yuan for as much as 45% of Nanjing airport, from which Singapore Airlines [19] has fifth freedom rights to operate cargo services to US destinations. BAA, the world's leading airport management company, has expressed interest in investing in secondary airports, which have international services and process a minimum of five million passengers annually (Orient Aviation [17]).

4   Low-cost carriers and regional airports

Southeast Asia's enormous populations, scattered land form, and growing economies have pushed LCCs into ascendancy. In most of Southeast Asia LCCs, shortly after initiating their businesses, quickly expanded to occupy a large percentage in the aviation market.

4.1   The rising of low-cost airlines

Following the experiences of LCCs in the US and the EU, the wave of LCCs that has emerged in Southeast Asia has raised expectations that the experience of LCCs in other major markets will now be replicated in this dynamic region. The main reason is that national airlines have often not been able to provide enough capacity, and they have often been criticized for their poor service standards in domestic markets (Chang and Lee [8]).

The aviation industry in Southeast Asia is always very competitive. Almost all of these Southeast Asian LCCs have been in business for only a few years, but they have expanded rapidly and now, particularly with the deregulation of the industry, own a large percentage of the aviation market in the region. Direct competition between full-service carriers (FSCs) and LCCs is intensifying across the area. Many evolving LCCs in Southeast Asia use several strategies which decrease its operation cost, promote efficiency, and attract passengers with low ticket price. This kind of airline business style immediately became popular with short-haul passengers.

4.2   Environmental Characteristics of Southeast Asia

Table 5 shows basic information of ASEAN countries. Enormous population is the most important characteristic of each of these ASEAN countries, and the population continues to grow. Another important standard used to describe these countries is the Gross Domestic Product (GDP). The GDP per capita in Southeast Asia is much lower as compared to other countries in the world. From 2005 to 2006, the GDP per capita in every country in ASEAN experienced positive growth. Table 6 contains information that describes communication, airports, and current airline businesses. Both the internet and cellular phone usage rates are low in these ASEAN countries, except Singapore. Cambodia, Burma, and Laos have a very low internet usage rate; it is even less than 1%.

The number of privately-operated airlines implicates the degree to which the aviation industry has the freedom to operate. In Malaysia and Cambodia, there is no state-operated airline. The governments of these two countries are the owners of their privately-operated airlines. Brunei, Burma, and Laos have no privately-operated airline. Therefore, the aviation industry in these three countries is less regulated. Airports are also important to aviation industry. Runway length over 1,524 m is acceptable for Airbus 320, one of the most widely used aircrafts of LCCs. The more airports with runways longer than 1,524 m a country has, the propitious condition to develop LCCs it becomes.

Table 5: Basic information of ASEAN countries.

	Total area (km^2)	Capital city	Population[1]	Population growth rate (%)[2]	GDP per capita(US$)[1]	Real GDP growth rate (%)[2]
Malaysia	329,750	Kuala Lumpur	24,385,858	1.78	1,700	5.3
Thailand	514,000	Bangkok	64,631,595	0.68	8,300	4.5
Singapore	692.7	Singapore	4,492,150	1.42	28,100	6.4
Indonesia	1,919,440	Jakarta	245,452,739	1.41	3,600	5.6
Vietnam	329,560	Hanoi	84,402,966	1.02	2,800	8.4
Philippines	300,000	Manila	89,468,677	1.80	5,100	5.1
Brunei	5,770	Bandar Seri Begawan	379,444	1.87	23,600	1.7
Cambodia	181,040	Cambodia Phnom Penh	13,881,427	1.78	2,200	6
Burma	678,500	Yangon	47,382,633	0.81	1,700	2.9
Laos	236,800	Vientiane	6,368,481	2.39	1,900	7.2

Note: [1]in July, 2006; [2]from 2005 to 2006. Source: CIA: The World Factbook [9].

Southeast Asia seems less developed than other areas in the world; however, it seems to have more tourism attractions. Many ASEAN countries continue their focus on the tourism industry. Table 7 presents the total tourism and visitor arrivals to ASEAN countries in 2005. Excluding Thailand and Indonesia, the total international visitor arrivals have increased in the remaining countries, with most of the visitors coming from other ASEAN countries. As Figure 6 demonstrates, 45% of the visitors are from ASEAN countries and an additional 27% from other Asian countries. This indicates that the main tourism market for Southeast Asia is from the Asia region. This implies that there is a good demand for regional airports for these visitors.

Table 8 provides basic information about some Southeast Asian LCCs. Most of them are subsidiaries of FSCs. Because of this close relationship, the Southeast Asian LCCs might not be operating as a true LCCs because there is bound to be legacy influence in the operation. The parent companies do not want to turn their subsidiaries into competitors, so the subsidiary LCCs and parents FSCs often do not share the same routes. For example, some of the subsidiaries only operate the domestic routes, or have only few international routes which connect to the major cities. Passengers sometimes are forced to use FSCs and pay more for the tickets. Non-subsidiary LCCs, such as AirAsia and LionAir [13], however, are not only willing to compete with FSCs, but to surpass them.

Table 6: Communication, airports, and aviation business in ASEAN countries.

	Communication		Airports		Aviation business	
	Internet usage rate %	Cellular phone usage rate% (about)	Number of airports	Number of runways length >1524 m	State-operated	Privately-operated
Malaysia	41.17	59.92	37	22	0	4
Thailand	13.03	42.36	66	41	1	15
Singapore	53.91	94.76	9	7	1	5
Indonesia	7.33	12.22	159	69	3	32
Vietnam	6.95	5.88	26	24	1	2
Philippines	8.74	36.81	83	37	1	14
Brunei	14.76	36.11	1	1	1	0
Cambodia	0.30	3.59	6	4	0	8
Burma	0.13	0.20	21	19	1	4
Laos	0.33	8.17	9	6	1	0

Source: CIA: The World Factbook, 2006; wikipedia airline list, http://en.wikipedia. org/wiki/Main_Page

Table 7: Tourism in southeastern countries.

	Total visitor arrivals	Percentage total visitor arrivals growth 2004~2005	ASEAN visitor arrivals	Percentage visitors from ASEAN	Risk of infectious diseases
Malaysia	16,431,055	4.43	12,984,646	79.03%	√
Thailand	11,516,936	−1.91	3,099,569	26.91%	√
Singapore	8,942,408	6.34	3,341,392	37.37%	
Indonesia	5,002,101	−5.84	2,038,292	40.75%	√
Vietnam	3,467,757	15.57	469,536	13.54%	√
Philippines	2,623,084	12.65	179,386	6.84%	√
Brunei	127,142	6.51	76,156	59.90%	
Cambodia	1,421,615	25.77	219,579	15.45%	
Burma	660,206	0.50	51,705	7.83%	
Laos	1,095,315	18.31	794,044	72.49%	
Total	51,287,619	4.35	23,254,305	45.34%	

Source: CIA: The World Factbook, 2006.

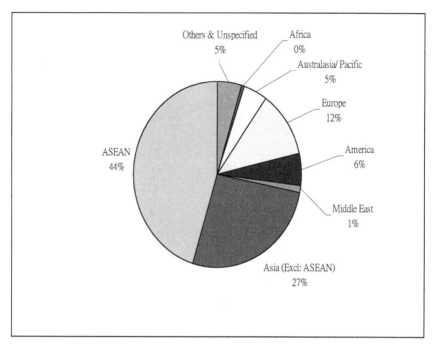

Figure 6: Visitor arrival % from each area.
Source: ASEAN official website [6].

Table 8: Basic information of some Southeast Asian LCCs.

LCCs company	Started year	Country	Base	Destinations
AirAsia	Dec. 2001	Malaysia	Kuala Lumpur International Airport	46
Cebu Pacific [7]	Mar. 1996	Philippines	Manila Ninoy Aquino International	40
Jetstar	May. 2004	Singapore	Singapore Changi Airport	–
Tiger Airways [20]	Dec. 2003	Singapore	Singapore Changi Airport	15
LionAir	Jan. 2000	Indonesia	Colombo Airport	–
Nok Air	Jul. 2004	Thailand	Bangkok Don Muang Airport	6
One-two-go	Dec. 2003	Thailand	Bangkok Don Muang Airport	–

4.3 Interaction of low-cost carriers and regional airports

Low-cost carriers in the Western countries often place destinations in smaller airports only. Most of them also need no air-bridges, have large negotiation space towards some regional small airports. Southeast Asian LCCs cannot use only regional small airports because there are only few airports that can be used in these ASEAN countries. The LCCs set destinations at the same airports with other FSCs. But there is still another alternative. The two main international airports, Changi Airport Singapore and Kuala Lumpur Airport Malaysia, always compete with each other. They both had their low-cost terminals launched in March 2006. These low-charged terminals are opened to attract LCCs which bring millions of tourists.

AirAsia is based in Malaysia, is by far the largest LCCs in Southeast Asia, and it is also the first LCCs in all Asia. It has 46 destination flied from Malaysia (Figure 7). Currently it planned a new LCCs airport for the capital Kuala Lumpur, it will be dedicated for use and managed by AirAsia, equipped with its own runway and air traffic control facilities. It is due to open in 2011. AirAsia transformed from a negative-revenue FSC and has not only turned from loss to profit, but also funded two subsidiaries, Thai AirAsia and Indonesia AirAsia. Its success suggests that the low-cost model could be a path to the victory in the Southeast Asia aviation competition.

Figure 7: Routes of AirAsia from Kuala Lumpur.

Source: AirAsia website [1].

Macau is one of the places, where AirAsia is considering establishing a joint-venture. The airline group currently operates to seven destinations in northeast Asia but Macau is by far its largest destination in terms of number of flights. AirAsia operates to Macau from four points in Malaysia and Thai AirAsia operates to Macau from Bangkok. AirAsia is looking at establishing an airline in the Philippines and has planned to establish an LCCs in Vietnam in joint-venture partnership with state-owned Vietnam Shipbuilding Industry Corp. But Vietnam already has three airlines. The government there has granted preliminary approval for two more and has said that in the near term it will cap the number of airlines operating in the country to five.

Towards the end of this year it is launching services to Perth in Australia after it receives a second A330. Also this year the airline plans to launch services to a second destination in China and a destination in India, a destination in South Korea and a destination in Taiwan.

5 Conclusions

Countries in Asia are more diverse politically, economically, and culturally than those in North America and Europe, with each of them differing in their approach to deregulation. Some countries, with strong economies and successful, well-established, national airlines, developed countries with small populations, and countries that are isolated, have been strong advocates of liberalization, while others have been fearful of the consequences. The economic characteristics in Asia included developed countries (Hong Kong, Japan, Korea, Singapore, and Taiwan) and developing countries (China, Indonesia, Malaysia, Philippines, and Thailand). Asian airport operators will be facing a challenging time ahead with air traffic growth at a reduced pace and volatility in fuel prices affecting airline business. In addition, the LCCs continuing growth in Asia, consumer need for point-to-point travel and scarcity of secondary airports in Asia have opened up many opportunities for airport operators and investors.

The strong economic development in China with an emerging middle and upper class has really stimulated air traffic demand. There were 142 airports that served civil aviation in China in 2005. On 4 July 2008, regular non-stop passenger flights between China and Taiwan have begun, nearly 60 years after the two sides split following a civil war. Under the agreement, airlines from each side are allowed to a total of 60 cargo flights per week. Flights are allowed to 7 Taiwanese airports and 21 Chinese Airports. It is expected the traffic will grow strongly in these airports in future in large part due to the new tourist demand.

In 2006, China's Total operations (international and domestic) ranked 2 in terms of Passenger-kilometres. This placed an enormous strain on the capital requirements of the commercial aviation sector. The Chine government concluded that its airlines and airports need capital and operational expertise; therefore, the CAAC opened its commercial aviation market to foreign investors. Afterwards, Copenhagen Airport has acquired 20% of the Haikuo Meilan International Airport Company, Aeroports de Paris acquired a 9.9% share in the Beijing Capital International Airport Co., German airport operator, Fraport A.G., took a 25% stake in Ningbo International airport, and Singapore Changi International Airport acquired 45% of Nanjing airport. BAA, the world's leading airport management company, also has expressed interest in investing airports in China. The equity investment with Chinese airports will help these European airports and Asian airport enter into China market.

There are lots of airports in Asia, it is not easy to collect the information of regional airports. Among Asian nations, Indonesia is first in its dependence on air transport. In these regional airports, some are popular tourist island airports, like Haikou of China, Bali of Indonesia, Jeju of Korea, Okinawa of Japan, Langkawi of Malaysia, and Phuket of Thailand. Because of their weather and beach, these island airports attract lots of passengers each year. In addition, in some countries, after some new hub airports operated, the old capital airport was transferred into regional function, including Japan's Tokyo Haneda Airport, Korea's Seoul Gimpo Airport, Taiwan's Taipei Shengshan Airport, Thailand's Bangkok Don Muang Airport, and China's Shanghai Hongqiao Airport.

The landforms of ASEAN are almost islands. Some archipelagic states, like Malaysia, the methods to travel from one island to another are only by through sea and air. In general, travel by air can save more time. Over the past decade, many new LCCs have arisen in Southeast Asia. Currently, Southeast Asia's enormous populations, scattered landforms, and their growing economies of the countries they service have pushed LCCs into ascendancy. Since the slogan of most LCCs is 'make all the people fly', travel by LCCs may be more efficient. AirAsia is by far the largest LCCs in Southeast Asia, it is based in Malaysia and has joint venture airlines in Indonesia and Thailand. It is looking at establishing an airline in the Philippines and planned to establish an LCCs in Vietnam.

While the 21st century has begun with an economic downturn both in the air transport market and in general, the cataclysmic events of 11 September, the Iraq war and SARS in some Asian countries have made this situation worse. The aviation industry is facing the most difficult economic situation it has ever experienced; even worse than the Gulf War in the 1990s. Although Asia-Pacific has been the fastest growing air travel market in the world during the last two decades, air transport deregulation and liberalization in the region has been slower than in North America and Europe. In the meantime, the ASEAN summit plans to open skies from capital city to capital city in 2008. In 2010, the member countries will open skies of a 'capital city +1', which means, besides capital cities, each member country will open an airline in one additional city. From that point on up to 2015, the member countries will achieve 100% open skies in the ASEAN region. As a result, other non-ASEAN countries in Asia should try to cooperate with the ASEAN members, to develop the Asian market into a Single Market, just like the EU did two decades ago. Once the air transport is deregulated, the airlines can compete to occupy the market without any restrictions. The regional airports will develop dramatically as a result of the liberalized market.

References

[1] Airasia, http://www.airasia.com.

[2] Airline Business, Japan expands Haneda internationalization, July, 2008.

[3] Air Transport Intelligence Database, www.rati.com.

[4] Air Transport World, World Airport Report, September, pp. 30–63, 2008.

[5] ASEAN Statistics, Tourist arrivals in ASEAN by selected partner country/region, http://www.aseansec.org/Stat/Table29.pdf (accessed Dec. 29, 2006).

[6] ASEAN Transport Action Plan 2005–2010, ASEAN official website, http://www.aseansec.org/16596.htm.

[7] Cebu Pacific, http://www.cebupacificair.com.

[8] Chang, Y.-C. and Lee, N., Are low-cost carriers a bargain? The comparison of low-cost and full-service carriers in southeast Asia. *Journal of the Transportation Research Board*, **2052**, pp. 21–27, 2008.

[9] CIA: The World Factbook, https://www.cia.gov/cia/publications/factbook/index.html.

[10] Dempsey, S.P., Airport Planning and Development Handbook: A Global Survey, New York: McGraw-Hill, 1999.

[11] International Civil Aviation Organisation (ICAO), Outlook for air transport to the year 2025, Montreal, 2007.

[12] Jetstar, http://www.jetmail.com.au.

[13] LionAir, http://www.lionair.co.id.

[14] Malaysia Airlines, http://www.malaysiaairlines.com.

[15] Nok Air, http://www.nokair.com/NokConnext/aspx/Welcome.aspx.

[16] One-two-go, http://www.fly12go.com.

[17] Orient Aviation, China: New era, new airports, June, 2006.

[18] Patel, M., Low cost airlines in Asia Pacific: Will it succeed or fail in this region? Travel Consulting Group, 2003.

[19] Singapore Airlines, http://www.singaporeair.com.

[20] Tiger Airways, http://www.tigerairways.com.

4

Air demand modelling: overview and application to a developing regional airport

M. Nadia Postorino
University 'Mediterranea' of Reggio Calabria, Italy

Abstract

Air demand forecast at airports is an important problem for the airport management and also for the regulator that has to plan a homogeneous development of the overall transport system. The current tendency is towards airport privatization; then, the goal to increase the served demand is one of the most important together with the progress of non-aviation activities. The evolution of the air transport system both in terms of low-cost companies, that generally use regional airports, and new technologies (as regional jets) has given a further impulse to the development of planning methodologies able to support decisions for an efficient distribution of resources. Regional airports can play an important role in this new background if the most suitable developing strategies are identified. This chapter wants to give a general overview about the problem of the air demand modelling, both in terms of theoretical approaches and practical problems. Models are classified with respect to different criteria, and the most suitable models for each planning level are also identified. An application to a regional airport in Southern Italy is also presented in order to test some of the described approaches and to obtain practical indications about applied models and developing strategies to be used.

Keywords: air demand; air demand model classification; airport catchment area; time series models; random utility models.

1 Introduction

The estimate of transport demand has always been one of the most important stages in the transport system planning process and one of the most stimulating challenges for the analysts, because the dependence of demand on the overall socio-economic system (particularly, income and job activities on the territory) makes it difficult to obtain reliable values. On the other hand, the supply characteristics (as e.g. terminal capacity, parking size and runways in the case of an airport system) as well as their performances and profitability are strongly dependent on the predicted demand levels.

Significant overestimates or underestimates of future demand levels lead to wrong developing policies that can generate respectively: (a) uneconomic use of infrastructures and/or services; (b) quick worsening of the transport system performances due to infrastructures and/or service deficiencies compared with the actual demand levels.

Generally, the analysis and the simulation of an air transport system concern three macro-topics:

- estimate of the air transport demand and its distribution among several competitive airports;
- identification of the supply organization and its effects on the different actors (community, passengers, airports, airlines);
- forecast of the air transport services and their induced effects on the air demand as well as on the other actors working in the system.

The first two aspects are linked to the system simulation for a given scenario (current scenario or future hypotheses). The third aspect depends on the airline/airport decision policies, the profit analysis, the market conditions, and, last but not least, the political decisions aiming at the system development following social other than technical criteria.

The increase in the air transport demand in the last few decades, also helped by the deregulation policy, has had a major effect of increasing transport services offered by different air carriers and has resulted in increasing congestion levels both in the airways and at airports (Graham and Guyer [1]). As an immediate effect of deregulation, the service offered to users, in terms of trip organization and costs, has changed rapidly and various alliances and mergers have occurred, together with the emergence of new air carriers in the market. For users, deregulation has produced greater benefits due to airfare decrease and the opportunity to choose among more flights supplied by more air carriers (Cohas et al. [2]). Thanks to deregulation, various air carriers have the opportunity to offer their services along high-demand routes, new connections have arisen and fare reductions have been applied (ATAG [3]). Hence, there has been an increase in the demand level, especially for non-systematic reasons (e.g. in Europe a reduction of 15% in airfares has produced an increase of about 10% in the carried passengers, Italian Ministry of Transport [4]).

Demand variations depending on local aspects (such as the building of a new airport or the expansion of an existing one) represent another important factor in modelling air transport demand, as the use of hub-and-spoke systems means that each pole can be potentially connected to almost any other.

Air transport demand directly affects the planning of airport terminals in terms of ground services design (check-in/check-out points, waiting areas, facilities as restaurants, shops and so on). In order to properly design such areas, both the absolute demand and its temporal distribution are required. Furthermore, even the competitiveness among airlines plays an important role to define the demand distribution.

The above considerations show how important the demand characteristic analysis and its evolution in time are in order to design more effectively the service supplied by both airport managers and air carriers.

Reliability of the demand estimates depends on the kind of model and data availability. Models theoretically efficient in terms of forecast often require a lot of data referred to users and both socio-economic and supply systems for a long period of time in order to estimate not only the current demand characteristics but also the future levels. The knowledge of current and future levels helps planners to develop effective short-medium and long-term actions, respectively.

Thus, data availability and model reliability are the two key elements to obtain high-quality demand level forecast, within the effectiveness limits defined by the stability of the boundary conditions. The latter can be identified in the socio-economic and political stability, which has a relevant influence on the user's decisions to make trips and particularly to travel by aircraft.

In the following, the relationship between demand and airport catchment area is discussed (Sections 2), and a classification of the air demand approaches with respect to different criteria is proposed together with a description of the two most important air demand approaches (Section 3). Finally, after an overview of the Italian airport system (Section 4) an application to a regional airport located in Southern Italy is presented and discussed (Section 5).

2 Demand modelling and airport catchment area

A key element for evaluating the developing potentiality of airport systems, particularly regional airport systems, is the demand forecast for each airport serving the considered region; such a forecast should be consistent with the airport choices made by the air users travelling from and towards the region itself.

As it is well-known to transport analysts, demand forecast is a relevant input for the transport system planning; particularly, in the case of a regional airport, system forecasts of demand have a significant influence on the future functioning of each airport as well as on the development of the airport master plans.

Generally speaking, a demand model is a mathematical relationship linking the expected demand level (dependent variable) to one or more explanatory variables (independent variables), whose nature depends on the kind of model and the availability of the corresponding data.

The choice to start the air trip from a given airport can depend on many factors as accessibility, facilities, air services and connectivity levels (i.e. the destinations that can be reached from the airport itself). Accessibility depends on the land network available on the region, while the other factors depend on the airport characteristics and the airline supply.

For each airport, a catchment area is usually defined. In the literature, there are several definitions for airport catchment area, depending on the geographical or demand considerations.

Basically, from a geographical point of view, the airport catchment area can be defined as the area containing all the potential users and the passengers of a given airport (Transport Canada [5]). From a demand point of view, the airport catchment area can be defined as the number of travellers using a given airport, where origins of travellers can be identified in a surrounding study area whose size depends on the characteristics of the airport itself, but that does not necessarily represent the geographical extension of the airport catchment area. Both points of view lead ultimately to the knowledge of demand and geographical area.

The identification of the catchment area following either the first or the second point of view can be made by using different approaches and different models. Basically, the geographical point of view is better satisfied by using indicators (mainly, accessibility indexes) while the demand point of view is better satisfied by using behavioural models.

The geographical identification can be useful for airports not built yet, and then to estimate the airport's potential attractiveness just in terms of accessibility for users living in the surrounding area, given that the airport characteristics as well as the airline supply are not defined.

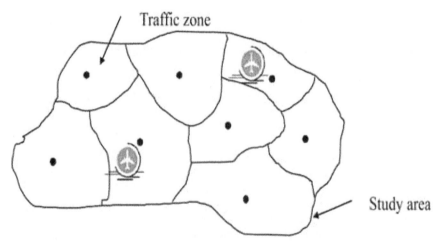

Figure 1: Airport catchment area identification: Study area and traffic zone.

The demand point of view can be useful when there are competitive airports and then it is crucial to establish which demand is considered while choosing a particular airport based on its characteristics. In this case, a study area containing an examined airport, and where more airports can be located, is identified and divided into traffic zones. The probability that users living in each zone and travelling by air choose that airport will depend on the characteristics of the airport itself and the competitive airports, as well as the distance (or, more generally, the accessibility measures) between each traffic zone and the examined airport [6, 7, 8, 9]. Then, the demand obtained at each airport represents the catchment area from the demand point of view, while its geographical identification potentially corresponds to the study area (Figure 1).

Furthermore, a distinction can be made between primary and secondary airport catchment areas (Transport Canada [5]). For a given airport, the first one refers to air travellers choosing that airport because they are 'captive'. The second one refers to air travellers that *may* choose that airport but are not captive and then are more elastic with respect to the choice of another airport (Figure 2). Generally, the secondary catchment area is typical both for airports where there are low-cost airlines and for classes of users that are more price-sensitive.

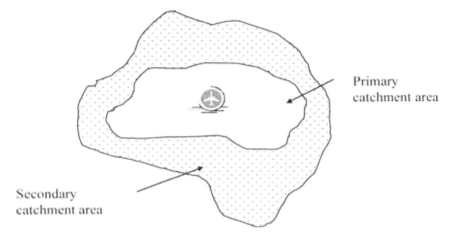

Figure 2: Primary and secondary airport catchment area.

Whatever be the approach, the knowledge of the airport catchment area is important because it represents the possible demand for the airport and then the potential for airport development. Demand levels and airport catchment area are then highly dependent on each other and land accessibility plays an important role.

As it is well-known in the economic and social sciences, accessibility is the key to development and particularly for airports. In fact, the larger the catchment area the larger the potential demand at the airport. An important factor for a successful airport development, mainly for regional airports, is to increase the catchment area other than providing good services in terms of fares, destinations and frequencies.

The simplest method to identify the geographical extension of the catchment area is to define a threshold value with reference to one or more accessibility indexes: the geographical area whose accessibility index is less than the threshold value is the airport potential catchment area; in other words, it contains the potential users and passengers of the airport. On a first approximation, the catchment area can be identified as the geographical area not larger than a prefixed time value (as 2 hours by car, for some important European airports (van Reeven, de Vlieger and Karamychev [10]) or 60 minutes by any land vehicles in the USA (Milone *et al.* [11])).

The knowledge of the geographical origin of passengers is a useful piece of information for the airport management in order to identify the best developing strategies; for example to decide if it is more suitable to invest on land accessibility rather than on airport facilities and services. Such knowledge can be achieved by running sample surveys on departing air travellers at the airport.

The key elements that can play an important role for the development of an airport can be identified as:

- capability to generate demand in the airport catchment area;
- capability to generate adequate demand (from the point of view of economic convenience) for potential point-to-point links;
- capability to adapt the airport services to the need and exigencies of the airlines;
- involvement of airlines on airport investments to improve the offered services.

In terms of factors affecting the size of the airport catchment area, and with reference to the primary catchment area only, the most relevant are:

- living population;
- yearly average income and average family income;
- employment level;
- sector of employment.

Generally, if the first three factors increase, the number of air travellers increases (and then the catchment area); while the distribution of sectors of employments is a useful indication to identify the potential air travellers by trip purpose (e.g. business travellers).

Furthermore, the airport catchment area also has an important impact on the financial situation of the airport itself. For example, airports surrounded by densely populated catchment areas and increasing population with employment levels and income in the average or over the average and employment sectors that generate business trips, generally, have got positive financial situations. An important role is also played by competition among airports; airports far away from the main national airports (250 kilometres following some studies on the Canadian regional airports [5]), where there are low-cost airlines, and that are also at a proper distance from the potential competing airport (e.g. 90 minutes by car) have still a good financial situation. On the other hand, airports offering similar services and sharing the same catchment area within a radius of about 100 kilometres, probably will have both a critical and negative financial situation.

The airport development also depends on the location of other, potentially competitive, airports. In the current situation, airports play a competitive role rather than a cooperative one and then the distance among airports as well as the services offered are crucial in terms of user choices. Generally, users are willing to cover longer distances to obtain better trip fares, point-to-point flights, larger choice sets of available airlines and flights to choose the best options in terms of departure time, destination and airline reliability (Suzuki [12]).

Furthermore, the presence of fast land modes (as fast trains) that can be competitive in terms of fares and times with respect to the destinations served at the airports can be an additional important factor in the airport users' choice. Indeed, one of the EU topics of major interest is the analysis of the fast train network influence on the distribution of traffic volumes among airports; land fast links between city pairs are supposed to produce a decrease in the air transport demand among the same city pairs (Button [13]). However fast trains also represent an easy way to arrive quickly at major airports (e.g. the Inter City Express links between Frankfurt and Paris or the international high speed trains linking Paris and Brussels to Great Britain trough the Channel Tunnel) and then they also contribute to improve the airport catchment area in a whole, integrated and inter-modal transport system. The complexity of the fast train role (competition or integration?) with respect to airports is one of the most attractive research fields in the transport system analysis.

3 Demand model classification

Passengers demand models can be classified with reference to the transport system representation, the mathematical formulation, the nature of variables (Table 1).

Table 1: Demand model classification.

Zone approach	Multi-mode models	Stage models (discrete choice)	
		Static models	Competitive Non-competitive
	Uni-mode models	Stage models (discrete choice)	
		Time series models	Competitive Non-competitive
Airport pairs approach	Uni-mode models	Static models	Competitive Non-competitive
		Time series models	Competitive Non-competitive

First of all, a distinction can be made between air demand models providing forecasts for specific city-pairs, corresponding to airport-pairs serving those cities, and demand models providing forecasts for O–D pairs, corresponding to traffic zones pairs. Whatever be the used approach, in the first case the focal point is the analysis of the specific relationship between airports or among one airport and all the others, while in the second case the demand model is usually part of a more general framework where demand is estimated for traffic zones and many transport modes; for the aircraft mode, demand is also allocated to one or more competitive airports by using suitable models (airport choice is described in Chapter 5).

Traditionally, demand models are classified as aggregate and disaggregate depending on the nature of data referred to demand and explanatory variables. If the variable 'demand' is referred to a single user, and so the explanatory variables, the model is said to be disaggregate, while if the variable 'demand', and then the explanatory variables, are referred to a homogeneous group of users the model is said to be aggregate.

Furthermore, models can be called: (1) descriptive or behavioural according to whether there are or not explicit hypotheses about trip user behaviour; (2) multi-mode or uni-mode if they allow obtaining mode shares among several alternative modes or demand on only one transport mode, respectively. Particularly, multi-mode models refer to the simulation of the overall transport system, where many transport modes are generally available (e.g. train, bus, car, aircraft), and then the demand on many transport modes can be computed. On the contrary, uni-mode models provide forecasts of demand for only one transport mode and then they are suitable for the simulation of a part of the overall transport system (e.g. the air transport system).

Multi-mode models are generally stage models, where more trip characteristics as destination, frequency, mode and so on can be simulated by using discrete choice models (a general overview is in [14, 15]).

Uni-mode models can be classified as static if they simulate air demand at a given time, time series if they simulate the demand trend for a given time period, or stage models if they simulate more trip characteristics but for a mode-specific demand.

Time series models can still be grouped as Simple Time Series (or univariate) and Causal Modelling (or multivariate). Simple Time Series approaches, among the most used to obtain air demand forecasts, consider the stochastic nature of an event does not vary in time and they simulate the demand trend without explaining the causes. In other words, explanatory variables are not considered. On the other hand, Causal Modelling models simulate demand in terms of cause-effect relationships, i.e. they associate explanatory variables to the observed demand by means of mathematical relationships linking independent variables (causes) to dependent variables (effects). Explanatory variables are generally referred to the examined mode, but characteristics of alternative modes (and, particularly, competitive modes as fast train with respect to aircraft) can also be considered by using suitable variables (mainly, level-of-service variables). From this point of view, uni-mode models can be classified, respectively, as non-competitive and competitive.

Demand forecast can be achieved at two different levels of detail: for long-term planning (strategic level) and for medium-short planning (tactical or operational level), where the difference is mainly due to the amount of required input data and the resulting level of output information.

At a strategic level (long term), the air demand forecast should support hypotheses about both airport development and investment plans for a medium-long period. Then, models able to simulate the expected demand levels as a function of the past realizations – all the boundary conditions being the same – can be more attractive. In other words, the demand trend is analysed under the hypothesis that the underlying conditions (as the socio-economic system and/or the transport supply system) are evolving with the same characteristics. If different developing scenarios in terms of socio-economic and/or transport supply systems can be tested, then specific hypotheses about the trend of the variables representing such scenarios should be made, in order to obtain expected demand levels consistent with them.

Models that better support the strategic planning are time series models that generally use aggregate information referred to the dependent and independent variables that occurred in a suitable time period (normally, at least 10 years).

At a tactical or operational level (medium-short time), the air demand forecast should support operational hypotheses about modifications of the system, particularly in terms of supply re-organization, with limited monetary investments. In this case, models should use explicitly explanatory variables simulating the supply characteristics (as frequency and/or departure times, fares, land services, airport accessibility, available land mode to reach the airport and so on) as well as user characteristics (as user type, age, trip purpose, family income and so on). In other words, the level of details should be compatible with the nature of the required demand estimate.

Models that better support the tactical and operational planning are discrete choice models; they require a greater level of detail, but can provide more information both about the expected characteristics of the air demand and the potential share between competitive, alternative modes (as aircraft and fast trains).

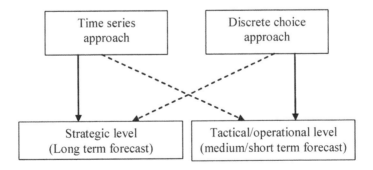

Figure 3: Approaches for air demand modelling and planning levels.

However, time series models and discrete choice models can be used at both planning levels (Figure 3), depending on the nature of the analysis and the data availability as well as the required output detail levels.

For example, discrete choice models can be used to test hypotheses about the development of the overall transport system, the air transport system being only a part of it, in relation to long-term planning projects as the building of fast speed railways or new road infrastructures. Similarly, time series models can be used to verify airport developing policies; for example the introduction of new links or variations in flight frequencies, for short term periods as 2–5 years.

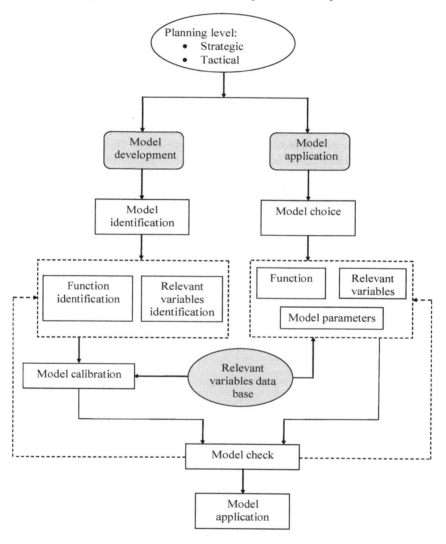

Figure 4: Model development and application.

Forecast of the air transport demand can also be referred both to a single airport inside a geographical (or administrative) region and to a set of airports inside a common area where they can be considered 'competitive' to each other. The choice to simulate the air demand only for one airport or to verify its distribution among two or more of them depends on the effective competition among airports, strongly linked to the identification of the airport catchment area.

Whatever be the planning level, the development and application of an air demand model requires three main steps (see also Figure 4):

- identification of the most suitable mathematical model able to simulate/forecast air transport demand with respect to the expected results and/or the prefixed goals;
- availability of data to calibrate the model parameters and to apply the model;
- check of the obtained model.

In the application stage, an available model can be used to simulate the air demand, the only care being the opportunity to use model parameters referred to similar socio-economic contexts. In this case, the check stage concerns the application of the model to a known situation in order to verify the congruence of the parameters, while in the case of model development the check stage refers to some statistical tests about the goodness of the estimated parameters and the statistical reliability of the overall model.

One important aspect concerning both the development and application of an air demand model is the data collection. Data referred to (air) transport demand concerning both user socio-economic characteristics and travel behaviour are often difficult to obtain. Generally, available data refer to official, aggregate statistics on boarded/de-planed passengers, pro-capita income for geographical/administrative regions and so on, but depending on the kind of model and detail required they can be inadequate to develop a suitable demand model.

Moreover, travel times and costs are the most relevant level-of-service variables introduced in a demand function. For air transport systems, travel times refer to flight duration, possible waiting time for connecting flights, boarding/disembarkation, baggage claim, and access/egress times. Costs mainly refer to monetary costs and generally to airfare.

Some data concerning airline supply can be difficult to obtain without specific surveys; particularly, airfare is the most difficult variable to quantify for at least two main reasons: (1) useful data are not always available and (2) there is a very large set of fares proposed by different air carriers and also inside the same air carrier. Actually, airfares can change significantly depending on many factors as the day on which the ticket is bought, the time period (week-end, particular days or months of the year and so on), the number of booked people, the age, the participation to flight programs (as frequent flier programs) and so on. When international trips are considered, the problem is still more complex because origins and/or destinations are in different countries with different currencies, while the fare has to be expressed in one reference monetary value, e.g. by using the exchange rate that, in turn, is variable during the year.

To overcome the problem by considering the quality of the offered service (and then, implicitly, the willingness to pay to use it), the hedonic pricing theory can be used (Rosen [16]). Its basic foundations are that users evaluate the characteristics of a good or the services it offers rather than the good itself. Following this approach, the observed fare can be considered as a function of the offered service and/or user characteristics; then, users are willing to pay according to the satisfaction they receive.

The following sections provide a brief overview of the main characteristics for both time series and discrete choice models.

3.1 Time series approach

Time series models to simulate air transport demand can have different levels of complexity depending on the general aims and the data availability for both model calibration and application. They have been largely used to predict air demand levels, see among others [17, 18, 19, 20, 21, 22, 23].

To briefly summarize, a time series is a stochastic process where the time index takes on a finite or countable infinite set of values. A stochastic process is an ordered and infinite sequence of random variables: if the time index t assumes only integer values, then it is a discrete stochastic process. To describe it, its mean and its variance are used as well as two functions: the AutoCorrelation Function (ACF) ρ_k, k being the lag, and the Partial AutoCorrelation Function (PACF) π_k, k being the lag. The ACF is a measure of the correlation between two variables composing the stochastic process, which are k temporal lags far away; the PACF measures the net correlation between two variables which are k temporal lags far away [24, 25].

AutoRegressive Moving Average (ARMA) models are a class of stochastic processes expressed as follows:

$$X_t - \sum_{i=1}^{p} \phi_i X_{t-i} = a_t - \sum_{j=1}^{q} \theta_j a_{t-j}, \tag{1}$$

where a_t is a White Noise process, ϕ and θ the model parameters, p and q the order of the AutoRegressive (AR) and Moving Average (MA) processes, respectively [24]. If the B operator such as $X_{t-1} = BX_t$ is introduced, the general form of an ARMA model can be written as follows:

$$\phi(B) \cdot X_t = \theta(B) \cdot a_t.$$

To estimate these models, some conditions should be verified: the series must be stationary and ACF and PACF must be time-independent. The non-stationarity in variance can be removed if the series is transformed with the logarithmic function. The non-stationarity in mean can be removed by using the operator $\nabla = (1-B)$ applied d times in order to make the series stationary. In this way, the ARMA model becomes an ARIMA (AR Integrated MA) model:

$$\nabla^d \phi(B) \cdot X_t = \theta(B) \cdot a_t. \tag{2}$$

This family of univariate models is largely used to obtain air demand prediction at a first level of knowledge and when no more data other than the demand time series is available. In this case, X_t represents the air demand at an airport i (or for an origin/destination pair i, or a traffic zone i) at time t, d_{it}:

$$\nabla^d \phi(B) \cdot d_{it} = \theta(B) \cdot a_t.$$

For a given set of data, the Box-Jenkins approach [24] is the most known method to find an ARIMA model that effectively can reproduce the data generating the process. The method requires three stages: identification, estimation and diagnostic checking.

Preliminarily, data analyses should be carried out in order to verify the presence of outliers. The identification stage provides an initial ARIMA model specified on the basis of the estimated ACF and PACF, starting from the original data:

- If the autocorrelations decrease slowly or do not vanish, there is non-stationarity and the series should be differenced until stationarity is obtained. Then, an ARIMA model can be identified for the differenced series.
- If the process underlying the collected series is a MA(q), then the ACF ρ_k is zero for $k > q$ and the PACF is decreasing.
- If the process underlying the collected series is an AR(p), then the PACF π_k is zero for $k > p$ and the ACF is decreasing.
- If there is no evidence for a MA or an AR then a mixture ARMA model may be adequate.

Several statistical tests have been developed in the literature to verify if a series is stationary, among these, the most widely used is the Dickey-Fuller test (Makridakis *et al.* [26]). After an initial model has been identified, the AR and MA parameters have to be estimated, generally by using least squares (LS) or maximum likelihood (ML) methods. The choice of the AR component order derives from the analysis of the PACF correlogram; for large sample size, if the order of the AR component is p, the estimate of the partial autocorrelations π_k are approximately normally distributed with mean zero and variance $1/N$ for $k > p$, where N is the sample size. The significance of the residual autocorrelations is often checked by verifying if the obtained values are within two standard error bounds, $\pm 2/\sqrt{N}$, where N is the sample size (Judge *et al.* [25]). If the residual autocorrelations at the first $N/4$ lags are close to the critical bounds, the reliability of the model should be verified. Another test that can be used is the Ljung and Box one [27]:

$$Q = N \cdot (N+2) \cdot \sum_{k=1}^{m} (N-k)^{-1} \cdot [\rho_{\hat{a}}(k)]^2,$$

where $\rho_{\hat{a}}(k)$ are the autocorrelations of the estimate residuals and k is a prefixed number of lags. For an ARMA (p, q) process this statistic is approximately χ^2

distributed with $(k–p–q)$ degrees of freedom if the orders p and q are specified correctly.

To check the residuals normality, the Jarque-Bera (JB) test [28] can be used:

$$JB = \frac{N - n_p}{6} \cdot \left(S^2 + \frac{(K-3)^2}{4} \right),$$

where S is a measure of skewness, K is a measure of Kurtosis, n_p is the number of parameters and N is the sample size. This test verifies if skewness and kurtosis of the time series are different from those expected for a normal distribution. Under the null hypothesis of normal distribution, the JB test is approximately χ^2 distributed with two degrees of freedom.

Models (1) or (2) use the past values of the examined variable to predict its future values. If some explanatory (or independent) variables are inserted in order to verify cause-and-effect relationships, the dependent variable X_t generally depends on lagged values of the independent variables and the model can be said multivariate. The length of the lag may sometimes be known a priori, but usually it is unknown and in some cases it is assumed to be infinite.

The simplest multivariate time series demand models are of the kind as follows:

$$d_{it} = \beta_0 + \beta^T y_{it} + u_{it},$$

$$u_{it} = \rho u_{i,t-1} + \varepsilon_{it},$$

where demand for an airport i (or for an origin/destination pair i, or a traffic zone i) at time t, d_{it}, is specified as function of n explanatory (and relevant) variables y_{it}. β^T are the unknown model parameters, β_0 the model constant, u_{it} a random term, ε_{it} a White Noise random residual and ρ the autocorrelation parameter taking into account the time dependence among the variables. The basic hypothesis is that the variable at year t is a function of the same variable at year $t–1$, as specified by the random term.

More general models can be obtained by starting from univariate ARIMA models and introducing more explanatory variables. Normally, if one dependent variable and one explanatory variable are considered, then the model has the form as follows:

$$d_{it} = \alpha + \beta_0 y_{it} + \beta_1 y_{i,t-1} + \ldots + \beta_P y_{i,t-P} + e_{it}, \tag{3}$$

under the hypothesis that $\beta_k = 0$ for k greater than a finite number P, called lag length. Models (3) are called finite distributed lag models, because the lagged effect of a change in the independent variable is distributed into a finite number of time periods.

If $e \sim (0, \sigma^2 I)$ and y_t are fixed, then, based on the sample information, the LS estimator is the best linear unbiased estimator for $(\alpha, \beta_0, \ldots, \beta_P)$. If the true lag length P is unknown but an upper bound M is known, then the LS estimator of $\beta = (\alpha, \beta_0, \beta_1, \ldots, \beta_M)^T$ is inefficient since it ignores the restrictions $\beta_{P+1} = \ldots =$

$\beta_M = 0$. In order to compute P, these sequential hypotheses can be set up as follows:

$$d_o(k_1, k_2, ..., k_n) = n_o \Pi_i p(k_i),$$

versus

$$H_a^m : P = M - m + 1, \Rightarrow \beta_{M-m+1} \neq 0 \left| H_0^1, H_0^2, ..., H_0^{m-1} \right.$$

The null hypotheses are tested sequentially beginning from the first one. The testing sequence ends when one of the null hypotheses of the sequence is rejected for the first time. The likelihood ratio statistic to test the m-th null hypothesis can be written as follows:

$$\lambda_m = \frac{\mathrm{SSE}_{M-m} - \mathrm{SSE}_{M-m+1}}{\hat{\sigma}^2_{M-m+1}},$$

where SSE_P is the sum of the squared errors for a model with lag length P. This statistic has an F-distribution with 1 and $(T - M + m - 3)$ degrees of freedom if H_0^1, H_0^2, H_0^m are true.

When the lag has been computed, the explanatory variable can be inserted in the univariate model, in order to derive a so-called multivariate ARIMAX model. In the general case of more than one explanatory variables, the model has the form as follows:

$$\nabla^d \Phi(B) \cdot d_{it} = \theta(B)_t \cdot a_t + \sum_{l=0}^{P_1} \beta_{t-l}^{(1)} y_{i,t-l}^{(1)} + \sum_{l=0}^{P_2} \beta_{t-l}^{(2)} y_{i,t-l}^{(2)} + ... \qquad (4)$$

where: $y_{t-l}^{(j)}$ is the j-th independent variable at time $(t-l)$ and $\beta_{t-l}^{(j)}$ is the corresponding parameter.

Figure 5 shows the different kinds of applications of air demand time series models, preferably for strategic planning levels.

Univariate models do not require explanatory variables but only the demand past 'history'; furthermore, they do not require the explicit identification of the airport catchment area but, for example, only boarded/de-planed passengers at the airport, time series data being available.

On the other hand, multivariate models present one or more explanatory variables as frequencies, income, number of employment and so on; some of them, as socio-economic variables, refer to the airport catchment area that has to be explicitly identified.

As Figure 5 shows, univariate and multivariate models can be used at aggregate and disaggregate levels; in the last case, the variables are defined for each traffic zone, demand generated by each traffic zone at year t can be estimated and then characterized as function of destination, departure time, transport mode and so on, by using discrete choice models (Section 3.2). Furthermore, mode-specific travel demand (as air demand) can be directly generated for each traffic zone, and again the other characteristics as destination and departure time as well as airport, airlines, access mode are simulated.

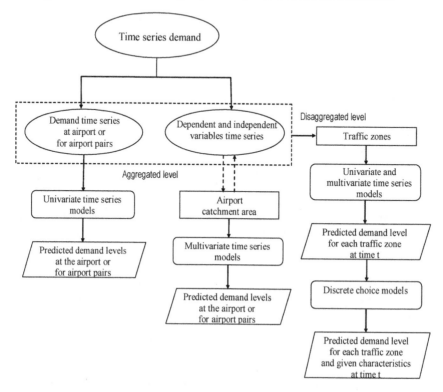

Figure 5: Application of time series models to estimate air travel demand.

3.2 Discrete choice models

Discrete choice models are a well-known class of models largely used in the transportation field to obtain trip demand specified with some characteristics as trip purpose, trip origin and destination, departure time, transport mode and so on [14, 15]. The most general form of a discrete choice multistage demand model is:

$$d_o(k_1, k_2, ..., k_n) = n_o \Pi_i p(k_i), \qquad (5)$$

where $d_o(k_1, k_2,..., k_n)$ is the travel demand with trip origin o and characteristics $k_1, k_2, ..., k_n$ that can be specified from time to time depending on the exigencies; n_o is the number of potential users in the origin o and $p(k_i)$ is the choice percentage referred to the characteristic (or choice dimension) k_i. They can be estimated by using simple statistical approaches or Random Utility Models (RUM).

To estimate the air demand by starting from model (5), suitable choice dimensions k_i and the corresponding $p(k_i)s$ should be identified, as in the following simple sequential specification:

$$d_{odh}(s,m) = d_o(sh)[\text{SE},\text{TS}] \cdot p(d/osh)[\text{SE},\text{TS}] \cdot p(m/odsh)[\text{SE},\text{TS}] \quad (6)$$

where SE and TS represent the vector of the socio-economic and territorial system characteristics, because the choice percentages depend on both user (socio-economic) and level-of-service/activity (territorial system) characteristics. Indexes o, d, h, s, m represent the trip dimensions, respectively, trip origin, trip destination, time period, trip purpose, trip travel mode, while $p(./..)s$ represent the choice probability (or choice percentage) for each choice dimension.

As models (6) shows, the order in the sequence also defines the dependence of each choice dimension on the previous one by means of suitable variables; the identification of the more suitable sequence is not a trivial task; particularly, for mode-related choices it is not easy to identify the best and more reasonable sequence to model the complex user behaviour concerning travel planning. For example, the choice to travel by aircraft implies also the choices of departure and arriving airports, the airport access/egress mode, the airline (e.g. traditional vs. low-cost); the latter can be simulated by means of suitable variables inside the mode choice dimension or within a decision process where the choice dimensions, their hierarchical order, if any, and their reciprocal effects should be simulated (more on airport choice is in Chapter 5).

In any case, the sequence (6) might be completely changed if the user choice process happens in a different way, e.g. users travelling for leisure, first of all, can decide to use an aircraft to start their trip and then make all the other mode-related choices, included the trip destination. On the other hand, if destination is compulsory (e.g. business travel), sequence (6) matches the decision process. In any case, the identification of the best sequence and then the best model is the result of a trial-and-error procedure.

Sequential discrete choice models as in eq. (5) have been used at national level to simulate the trip demand on many available transport modes, included aircraft, so as to define the best developing policies for the overall transport system by taking into account also its impact. This approach could be particularly useful to verify how much the overall transport system and each of its components are responsible for the greenhouse effects and which actions could be undertaken in order to satisfy the Kyoto protocol.

The hypotheses underlying a RUM approach to estimate the $p(./..)s$ suppose users are rational decision makers and they choose the best option among a set of available alternatives; such a choice is based on the random utility value associated to each alternative belonging to the choice set and depending on the characteristics (attributes) of the alternative itself and the other available alternatives. Then, users choose the option with the highest value of utility, and since utility is a random variable only the probability that users choose a specific alternative can be computed.

Starting from these hypotheses, many multistage RU discrete choice demand models can be identified by specifying choice dimensions, choice sequences and discrete choice models (Figure 6); whatever be the discrete choice model, its use requires: (1) the identification of the choice set; (2) the identification of the relevant attributes characterizing each alternative; (3) the identification of the mathematical form for the random utility variable [8, 29, 30, 31].

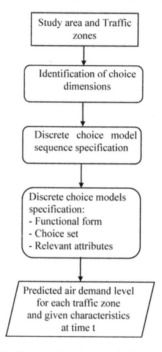

Figure 6: Steps in the discrete choice approach.

RUMs are a family of behavioural models trying to simulate user behaviour starting from some mathematical hypotheses. Recently, other paradigms have been proposed to understand user preferences, by using Neural Networks (NN) and fuzzy-NN approaches [32, 33, 34]. However, NN do not allow the explicit values of the parameters to be computed, so the interpretation of the model in terms of elasticity values, parameter ratios and so on cannot be obtained.

Estimation of the air demand requires more than the mode dimension because subsequent, relevant choices are also important, as the airport choice that allows obtaining the number of (potential) passengers at the airport, or the airport access mode in order to identify the needs of users and then identify solutions to offer suitable landside facilities.

4 An overview of the Italian airport system

Currently, the number of airports opened to civil and military aviation on the Italian territory is 115; among these, about 15 are military airports and the remaining can be classified half as commercial and half as general aviation.

Commercial airports refer to scheduled and charter flights, general and military aviation. General aviation airports usually have short runways and services are provided for medical and Civil Protection.

Following the EU classification, as shown in Table 2, in Italy there are 2 community airports (yearly passengers greater than 10 million), 5 national airports (yearly passengers from 5 to 10 million), 14 large regional airports (yearly passengers from 1 to 5 million) and 16 small regional airports (yearly passengers less than 1 million).

In recent years, the air demand in the Italian market has increased, following the general world tendency. According to forecasts provided by IATA and the European agency for the air transport safety (Eurocontrol), passenger volumes are expected to increase further in the future years; particularly, IATA [35, 36] predicts an average increase at a rate of about 3–4% starting from 2005, while Eurocontrol [37] predicts a yearly average increase in the European market at a rate of about 3% during the period 2005–2025. Anyway, short-medium trends are continuously revised due to contingent situations (as political stability, oil price and so on).

As for the Italian market, Eurocontrol forecasts a yearly average increase of about 2–3% for the domestic market, while international markets are expected to increase at a rate of about 4% for the next 8 years.

In the period 1997–2006, the annual passenger growth rate in the Italian market was about 6%; the Rome/Fiumicino-Milan/Linate pair has been the second busiest route within the EU market, with more than two million passengers carried (source: Eurostat, http://www.ec.europa.eu/eurostat).

The analysis of the current situation in the Italian air market shows a rather scattered demand, probably due to the relatively high number of commercial airports per square mile; at the same time, the absence of an effective and widespread land network that can guarantee a suitable accessibility to/from the airport (mainly regional airports but also many national airports) reduces the potential air demand. Furthermore, in many cases the average distances among airports are about 130–160 kilometres, supplied air services are often similar and small airports are in competition to capture demand from overlapping catchment areas.

In this context, an important role is also played by airlines and their relationships with airports. Starting from the liberalization of the air transport system in Europe, more than 30 new commercial airlines have risen in Italy, but today less than half is still in the market and most of them have a marginal market share. Routes between many Southern Italy regional airports and the main airports (Rome, Milan above all) are operated by a few airlines without a significant competitiveness among them, while for some others airports, specially located in Northern Italy, supply exceeds demand.

Many regional airports offer point-to-point international links, often operated by low-cost companies; many of them serve tourist destinations in Northern Italy (as Venice, Florence) but seasonal flights at lower costs are also starting for more decentralized regions (as Sardinia, Calabria), thus improving the tourist flows towards them. Low-cost airlines in Italy have a share of about 13% on the domestic market and about 30% on the international market.

The Italian international traffic is greater than domestic traffic: in 2007, the percentage of international passengers takes about 59% of the overall Italian market, while in the period 2004–2007 the number of passengers carried on international routes had an increase of more than 10%.

Table 2: Airport classification based on passengers traffic.

2006	IATA code	Pass. (arr.+dep.)	2005-2006 %var.	2006	IATA code	Pass. (arr.+dep.)	2005-2006 %var.
ROMA Fiumicino	FCO	29726051	5.4	GENOVA Sestri	GOA	1070459	6.7
MILANO Malpensa	MXP	21621236	10.9	ALGHERO Fertilia	AHO	1068040	-0.4
MILANO Linate	LIN	9693156	6.7	BRINDISI Papola Casale	BDS	816216	3.0
VENEZIA Tessera	VCE	6296345	8.9	TRIESTE Ronchi dei Leg.	TRS	665426	10.6
CATANIA Fontanarossa	CTA	5370411	3.9	FORLI'	FRL	620809	9.4
BERGAMO Orio al Serio	BGY	5226340	21.8	REGGIO CALABRIA	REG	578015	51.0
NAPOLI Capodichino	NAP	5056643	10.6	ANCONA Falconara	AOI	473701	1.3
ROMA Ciampino	CIA	4993487	16.8	PESCARA	PSR	333036	-0.8
PALERMO Punta Raisi	PMO	4246555	11.5	RIMINI Miramare	RMI	319702	18.9
BOLOGNA Borgo Panig.	BLQ	3928887	8.4	TRAPANI Birgi	TPS	313798	-20.2
TORINO Caselle	TRN	3215593	2.9	BRESCIA	VBS	225470	-43.6
PISA San Giusto	PSA	3002621	29.5	LAMPEDUSA	LMP	196604	-4.5
VERONA Villafranca	VRN	2961377	14.7	PANTELLERIA	PNL	152247	10.4
CAGLIARI Elmas	CAG	2464084	5.1	PARMA	PMF	122023	118.9
BARI Palese Macchie	BRI	1950857	20.1	CROTONE	CRV	104154	26.4
OLBIA Costa Smeralda	OLB	1765518	9.8	BOLZANO	BZO	68550	8.7
FIRENZE Peretola	FLR	1520320	-9.8	PERUGIA Sant'Egidio	PEG	42565	-18.9
LAMEZIA TERME	SUF	1341936	16.2	FOGGIA Gino Lisa	FOG	6714	7.8
TREVISO Sant'Angelo	TSF	1328288	3.1	ITALY	/	122889091	8.8

Source: ENAC – National Agency for Civil Aviation, Italy.

Critical aspects of the Italian air transport system are mainly the poor accessibility, the under-utilization of the potential capacity for many airports and a flight supply that sometimes does not match the transport demand needs.

To summarize, the Italian airport system situation is very heterogeneous, both from an operational and an economic point of view. The two larger airports (Rome Fiumicino and Milan Malpensa) gather the most part of the international traffic (Table 2), but some others have succeeded in creating a good international network that has increased the overall traffic volumes (as, e.g. the airports of Pisa, Rome Ciampino, Bergamo, Bologna). Finally, airports where low-cost carriers operate are also the most efficient, as it is expected, given the operational characteristics of low-cost carriers.

5 Application to a test case

Demand simulation at an airport by using time series models requires the knowledge of passengers and, possibly, explanatory variable time series data referred to the airport catchment area. RUM approaches can be preferred if an in-depth analysis has to be realized, particularly to understand the user behaviour with respect to airlines, airfares, airport characteristics and so on. However, some data are often difficult to obtain, particularly airfares. It is almost impossible to have authorized airfare data, they can be obtained indirectly by using IATA data, but information on discounted airfare is very limited. Finally, the application of RUMs often requires passenger data collected by means of suitable surveys, while time series models can use general data easier to obtain (as population, GDP and so on).

In any case, to have information on the air demand at an airport, as a starting point to understand the airport general trend and without specific analyses on the user choice behaviour, time series models can represent a useful tool.

The application refers to the airport of Reggio Calabria, in the South of Italy (Figure 7), located very near the city centre (about 5 kilometres), well connected to the main road network but weakly served by public systems (both buses and trains). Thanks to its position in front of the island of Sicily and near the Aeolian isles, it might become an important node of the Mediterranean transport system, particularly with reference to leisure traffic flows.

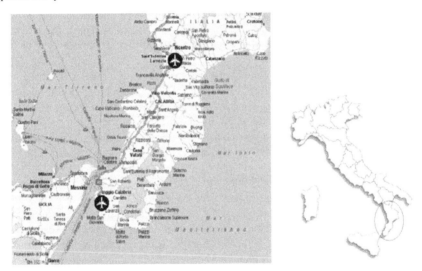

Figure 7:   Location of Reggio Calabria airport (Southern Italy) and its main competitive
            airport within the same administrative region.

The main competitive airport located in the same administrative region (Lamezia Terme) is about 140 kilometres far away. The second one, Catania Fontanarossa, is located in Sicily and the overall land distance is about 135 kilometres, but the access/egress time, included time spent to cross the Strait of Messina (between Sicily and Calabria), makes it less attractive to potential users.

As reported in Table 2, Lamezia Terme airport can be classified as a large regional airport and Catania as a national one, while Reggio Calabria is a small regional airport.

Starting from 2005, Reggio Calabria airport management has begun some developing policies by increasing the flight frequencies and the number of reached destinations. The new flights have been operated by some low-cost-like companies thus allowing lower fares for passengers. Before starting these developing policies, only hub-and-spoke flights were operated towards Rome and Milan by only two companies, one of them under a significant monopoly system. The new situation (more companies, more destinations both national and international, competition on some links) has had as consequence:

- the end of the monopoly system and then the opportunity to have more advantageous airfares;
- the opportunity to reach some destinations without transfer at hub(s);
- the increase of frequencies and the opportunity to choose among more destinations and for the same destination among more departure times and airfares.

The current situation is still in a developing but uncertain stage. In fact, the presence of the competitive Lamezia Terme airport, that is continuously expanding its supply and the served demand, makes the growth of the airport difficult, given also that its role in terms of both kind of services and reached destinations (and then market share) is not well defined if compared with the competing airport.

Furthermore, the airport catchment area, obtained by means of some RP surveys at the airport, is rather limited from a geographical point of view (Figure 8), the most part being concentrated around the city of Reggio Calabria (about 52% of demand is resident in the municipality area) and its province (about 30%), while a little part comes from the city of Messina (Sicily). Finally, a negligible percentage comes from the nearest provinces of the Calabria administrative region.

During the years 2005 and 2006, three surveys were conducted at Reggio Calabria airport, within the research project 'Methods and models to forecast the air passenger transport demand', part of a more general national project entitled 'Guidelines to plan the development of the Italian regional airports'. The goal of the surveys was to understand the main characteristics of users at the airports, to identify the catchment area and to have information on the airfare paid by users.

The first survey was realized immediately after the introduction of new links by new air companies, and the second one after some months during which more frequencies and more destinations were added. As Table 3 shows, the percentage of users in the price class 50–100 increases notably from the first to the second survey, while the percentage in the price class 0–50 is drastically reduced (really, this price class is linked to the initial launch bargain of new destinations with new companies). The increase of the percentage of users in the price class 50–100 is probably due to the presence of low-cost-like companies, that has had as an expected consequence the increase of competition on some routes and then a reduction of the average airfare.

The available, aggregate data refer to passengers and the main supply characteristics at the airports (as number of movements, frequencies, number of operating airlines and so on) for a given period (sources: Italian Official Statistic Institute ISTAT; Ministry of Infrastructure and Transport; Association of Italian Airports: www.assaeroporti.it).

Figure 8: Catchment area of Reggio Calabria airport.

Table 3: Comparison between the 1st and 2nd survey: Price class.

Price class (Euro)	Users [%] 1st survey	Users [%] 2nd survey
0–50	14.9	1.5
50–100	34.1	57.5
100–150	18.3	20.9
150–200	12.6	11.5
200–250	10.3	4.2
250–300	4.3	0.8
300–350	0.2	1.5
350–400	3.7	0.7
400–450	0.5	0.8
>450	1.1	0.5

Table 4 (and Figure 9) reports passengers data at the airport; note the outlier referred to 2004 when the airport was closed during the months of March, April and May for some adjustment work on the runway.

Table 4: Boarded/de-planed passengers at the airport of Reggio Calabria (period 1989–2007)*.

Year	Pax	Year	Pax	Year	Pax	Year	Pax
1989	157,225	1994	260,539	1999	543,041	2004	272,470
1990	245,711	1995	252,294	2000	538,048	2005	398,089
1991	222,571	1996	364,036	2001	481,857	2006	578,250
1992	246,306	1997	464,161	2002	463,662	2007	547,814
1993	266,782	1998	461,091	2003	441,795		

* Data have been collected by using more sources, as a unique data base does not exist.

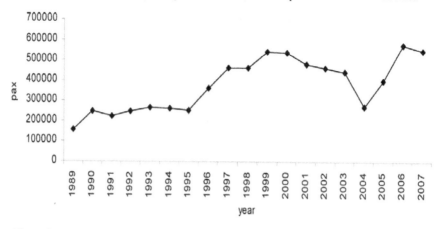

Figure 9: Passenger demand trend at the airport of Reggio Calabria (period 1989–2007).

After a positive trend from 1989 to 1999, the passenger demand has started to decrease systematically in successive years till 2004. The main reasons for this decrease are the progressive reduction of the supply and also the more and more expensive airfares. After 2004, the demand trend seems essentially positive, but the potential demand is probably higher even if a poor accessibility and the still uncertain developing policy at the airport stop its expansion.

Starting from the same boarded/de-planned passenger data base, both univariate and multivariate time series models have been calibrated.

Following the Box-Jenkins approach, some preliminary analyses have been carried out; estimated ACF and PACF for the boarded/de-planned passenger time series (Figure 10) show that ACF decreases linearly and the value of PACF at lag 1 is close to 1, i.e. there is mean non-stationarity that has been removed by differencing the series once. After that transformation, the Dickey-Fuller test applied to the differenced series confirms its stationarity. To remove the variance non-stationarity, the series has been transformed by using the logarithmic function. The estimate of the partial autocorrelation coefficients shows that only π_1 does not fall within the two standard error bounds $\pm 2/\sqrt{N}$ (Figure 10), so the order 1 can be established for the AR component. The same procedure is applied to choose the MA component order by using the correlogram of ACF, that suggests a MA(2) component. Then, from data analysis the identified general model is ARIMA(1,1,2):

$$(1-\phi B)\nabla \ln d_{tt} = c + (1 - \theta_1 B - \theta_2 B^2)a_t,$$

where c is the model constant.

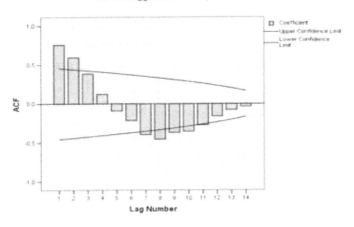

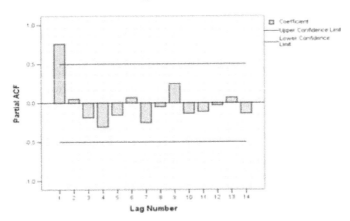

Figure 10: ACF and PACF correlograms.

Demand at year 2004 can be considered an outlier because the airport was closed during three months; then, to calibrate the model, the outlier has been suitably estimated in order to better follow the natural trend of the series. The model calibration has been carried out by using data till year 2005 while the remaining

2 years have been used as hold-out-sample to verify the model prediction capability (Figure 11).

A multivariate ARIMAX model has been calibrated too, by introducing some explanatory variables. As it is well known, the most powerful explanatory level-of-service variables to estimate transport demand are times and monetary costs, mainly airfares in this case. As said in Section 3, it is very difficult to obtain airfares, and especially for long time periods, but airfares are also one of the most interesting variables that can explain the air demand trend and its variations when the market conditions change (e.g. low-cost companies, competition on routes, within mode and between mode competitions and so on).

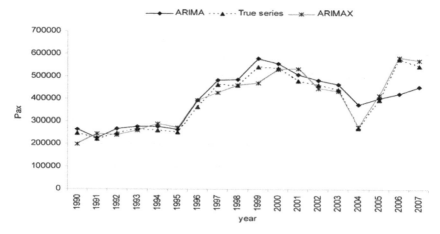

Figure 11: True and predicted air demand at the airport of Reggio Calabria – ARIMA and ARIMAX models.

As briefly described in Section 3, airfare can be estimated indirectly by using the hedonic pricing theory. Trip fare can then be expressed as follows:

$$F = f(a, b, ..., d),$$

where:

- F is the trip fare to move between two airports;
- f is a function to be specified;
- a, b, ..., d are user and/or trip characteristics as comfort, timetables, accessibility, delays, frequency and so on, which can be obtained by suitable surveys at airports.

In this case, function f has been specified in linear form, and the relevant variables are user average income, flight duration time, kind of air carrier and transfer waiting time (Table 5). All the data have been collected during the RP interview introduced before. The variable 'kind of air carrier' assumes value 1 if users choose the flag (or traditional) carrier and 0 otherwise. Time variables depend on the scheduled flights for the various legs and are expressed in hours. Finally, fares, transformed by using the logarithmic function, refer to one-way trips.

Table 5: Results of the fare model.

Variable	Coefficients	t-student (1%)
Income	0.88	23.93
Flight duration	1.45	26.88
Kind of airline	0.47	6.43
Waiting time	−0.82	−13.39
Statistical tests		
R^2	Adjusted R^2	
0.958	0.9579	

As Table 5 shows, all the parameters have correct signs and are statistically significant as well as the overall model (see R^2 and adjusted R^2). Users are willing to pay more for longer trips, but prefer direct flights or good connections, as the negative value of the waiting time variable suggests. Furthermore, despite a greater monetary cost they prefer flag carriers, probably due to the image of reliability and safety they inspire.

Generally, after the calibration of a fare model, its results can be used into a demand model as ARIMAX. In any case, even if this fare model specification has given good results in terms of descriptive power, for this application not all the time series data of the explanatory variables are available and then the fare model results cannot be used into an ARIMAX model. Then the explanatory variables considered here are the number of movements at the airport at year t, m_t, and the average per capita income at year t, I_t, that can be considered a proxy of the willingness to pay, and in some ways linked to the airfares at the airport. The number of movements is a level-of-service variable, representing the capability of the airport to offer flights, while income is a socio-economic variable depending on the activity system in the catchment area.

The sequential testing procedure described in Section 3.1 allows the P values for both variables to be identified; particularly, demand at year t depends on movements in the same year t and income from year t to year t–6. The resulting multivariate ARIMAX model is:

$$(1 - \Phi B)\nabla \ln d_t = (1 - \theta_1 B - \theta_2 B^2) \cdot a_t + \delta \cdot \ln m_t + \alpha_1 \ln I_t + \alpha_2 \ln I_{t-1} +$$
$$+\alpha_3 \ln I_{t-2} + \alpha_4 \ln I_{t-3} + \alpha_5 \ln I_{t-4} + \alpha_6 \ln I_{t-5} + \alpha_7 \ln I_{t-6} + \kappa.$$

The model has been calibrated by using data from 1989 to 2005, while the remaining data (2006–2007) were used as hold-out sample (Figure 11).

As Figure 11 shows, both ARIMA and ARIMAX models can well predict the air demand at the airport; years from 2005 to 2007, considered as hold-out sample, are better simulated by the ARIMAX model. Anyway, it is interesting to note that both models show good performances, although the theoretically most appealing multivariate model needs more explanatory variables to capture the demand trend. In some cases, the ARIMA model explains the demand trend better than the ARIMAX model. However, apart from the similar simulation capabilities, multivariate models can help to test possible developing policies by means of suitable hypotheses about the values of the explanatory variables. In this case, the level-of-service explanatory variable (movements) depends on the airport management and airline policies, while income depends on socio-economic developing policies, more complex and more difficult to estimate and control. Without specific developing policies on the territory and then all things being equal, income follows its trend, while hypotheses can be made on the number of movements in order to verify if and how demand can further increase.

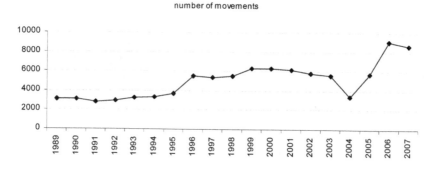

Figure 12: Number of movements trend at the airport of Reggio Calabria (period 1989–2007).

It is interesting to compare the trend of the number of movements (Figure 12) and passenger demand percentage variations at the airport (Figure 13) as well as the percentage variations with respect to 1999 (corresponding to the greatest demand value before 2005, when new companies began to operate at the airport). From Figure 13, it can be seen that the percentage variations of movements and passengers are rather similar, apart from the transition year 2005, when many developing policies started at the airport. More interestingly, Figure 14 shows the percentage variations with respect to the reference year 1999. In this case, till 2004 demand is decreasing quicker than the number of movements with respect to the reference year, but at a rather similar rate. After 2005, while the number of movements increases strongly, demand increases weakly and simply reaches the values already achieved at 1999.

The analyses of data thus suggest that the policies started at the airport do not capture the actual needs of passengers, as demand at years 2006–2007, practically equal to demand at year 1999, is satisfied by a supply really larger than that at the reference year. Then, even if the number of movements increases – suggesting more possible destinations, greater frequencies for the same destination, more flights at different times of the day – demand does not increase significantly with respect to the reference year 1999, when the number of movements was largely lower, but probably more suitable for the passengers needs.

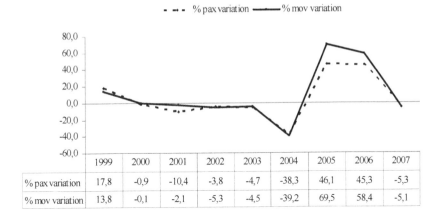

	1999	2000	2001	2002	2003	2004	2005	2006	2007
% pax variation	17,8	-0,9	-10,4	-3,8	-4,7	-38,3	46,1	45,3	-5,3
% mov variation	13,8	-0,1	-2,1	-5,3	-4,5	-39,2	69,5	58,4	-5,1

Figure 13: Number of movements and passenger demand percentage variations at the airport of Reggio Calabria.

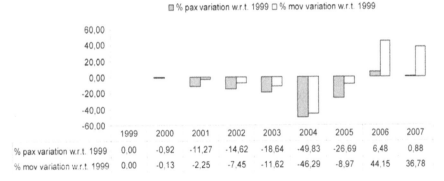

	1999	2000	2001	2002	2003	2004	2005	2006	2007
% pax variation w.r.t. 1999	0,00	-0,92	-11,27	-14,62	-18,64	-49,83	-26,69	6,48	0,88
% mov variation w.r.t. 1999	0,00	-0,13	-2,25	-7,45	-11,62	-46,29	-8,97	44,15	36,78

Figure 14: Number of movements and passenger demand percentage variations at the airport of Reggio Calabria with respect to year 1999.

To simulate the relationship between demand needs and air supply, probably the time series model should use more level-of-service explanatory variables taking into account not only the amount of supply but its distribution and its specific characteristics. However, when the required level-of-detail increases, data are more difficult to obtain, as official agencies at national and international level (as Eurostat) generally provide considerably aggregate data. Then, specific surveys have to be carried out that also allow combined time series and RUM to be used.

As the application at the regional airport of Reggio Calabria has showed, the regular collection of data at a given airport can be of great importance for the airport management, helping them to identify the best developing strategies, particularly when competition between airports exists. In this case, the decrease in demand despite the increase in the flight number can be due to the superior supply at the nearest competing airport, that in fact has strongly increased its demand, probably becoming attractive for people initially being in the Reggio Calabria airport catchment area.

From a modelling point of view, the results obtained with both univariate and multivariate time series models do not allow asserting that univariate models are better than multivariate models and vice versa. As obtained in this study, the better forecasting power of the univariate model is offset by its limits of validity, which depends on the stability of the boundary conditions. Multivariate models solve this problem by using explanatory variables, whose time series, however, are often difficult to find. Thus, the potential explanatory power of multivariate time series models is limited by the lack of suitable data.

References

[1] Graham, B. & Guyer, C., Environmental sustainability, airport capacity and European air transport liberalization: Irreconcilable goals? *Journal of Transport Geography*, **7(3)**, pp. 165–180, 1999.
[2] Cohas, F., Belobaba, P. & Simpson, R., Competitive fare and frequency effects in airport market share modelling. *Journal of Air Transport Management*, **2(1)**, pp. 33–45, 1995.
[3] Air Transport Action Group (ATAG), The economic & social benefits of air transport, September 2005, www.atag.org.
[4] Italian Ministry of Transport, *National Transport Analysis*, Rome: Istituto Poligrafico di Stato, 1998.
[5] Transport Canada, Regional and Small Airports Study (TP 14283B), 2004.
[6] Harvey, G., Airport Choice in a Multiple Airport Region. *Transportation Research*, **21A(6)**, pp. 439–449, 1987.
[7] Ashford, N. & Benchemam, M., Passengers' choice of airport: An application of the multinomial logit model. *Transportation Research Record*, **1147**, pp. 1–5, 1987.
[8] Hess, S. & Polak, J.W., Mixed logit modelling of airport choice in multi-airport regions. *Journal of Air Transport Management*, **11(2)**, pp. 59–68, 2005.
[9] Fuellhart, K., Airport catchment and leakage in a multi-airport region: The case of Harrisburg International. *Journal of Transport Geography*, **15(4)**, pp. 231–244, 2007.
[10] Van Reeven, P., de Vlieger, J. & Karamychev, V., BOB airport accessibility pilot, final report within the Fifth Framework Program for research, technological development, Erasmus University Rotterdam, Transport Economics Dept, 2003.
[11] Milone, R., Humeida, H., Moran, M., Seifu, M. & Hogan, J., FY-2003 Models development program for COG/TPB travel models, Metropolitan Washington Council of Governments, National Capital Region Transportation Planning Board, 2003.

[12] Suzuki, Y., Modelling and testing the 'two-step' decision process of travellers in airport and airline choices. *Transportation Research*, **43E(1)**, pp. 1–20, 2007.

[13] Button, K., The European market for airlines transportation and multimodalism, Airports as multimodal interchange nodes, Economic Research Centre, European Conference of Ministers of Transport 2005, http://internationaltransportforum.org/europe/ecmt/pubpdf/05RT126.pdf.

[14] Cascetta, E., *Transportation Systems Engineering: Theory and Methods*, Kluwer: The Netherlands, 2001.

[15] Ben Akiva, M. & Lerman, S., *Discrete Choice Analysis*, Cambridge, MA: MIT Press, 1985.

[16] Rosen, S., Hedonic prices and implicit market: Product differentiation in pure competition. *Journal of Political Economy*, **82**, pp. 34–55, 1974.

[17] Hensher, D.A., Determining passenger potential for a regional airline hub at Canberra International Airport. *Journal of Air Transport Management*, **8(5)**, pp. 301–311, 2002.

[18] Andreoni, A. & Postorino, M.N., A multivariate ARIMA model to forecast air transport demand. *Proc. of the European Transport Conference 2006*, www.aetransport.org.

[19] Inglada, V. & Rey, B., Spanish air travel and September 11 terrorist attacks: A note. *Journal of Air Transport Management*, **10(6)**, pp. 441–443, 2004.

[20] Karlaftis, M.G. & Papastavrou, J.D., Demand characteristics for charter air-travel. *International Journal of Transport Economics*, **XXV(3)**, pp. 19–35, 1998.

[21] Lim, C. & McAleer, M., Time series forecasts of international travel demand for Australia. *Tourism Management*, **23(4)**, pp. 389–396, 2002.

[22] Lai, L. & Lu, L., Impact analysis of September 11 on air travel demand in the USA. *Journal of Air Transport Management*, **11(6)**, pp. 455–458, 2005.

[23] Melville, J.A., An empirical model of the demand for international air travel for the Caribbean region. *International Journal of Transport Economics*, **XXV(3)**, pp. 313–336, 1998.

[24] Box, G.E.P. & Jenkins, G.M., *Time-Series Analysis, Forecasting and Control*, San Francisco: Holden-Day, 1970.

[25] Judge, G.G., *Introduction to the Theory and Practice of Econometrics*, 2nd edition, New York: Wiley & Sons, 1988.

[26] Makridakis, S., Wheelwright, S.C. & Hyndman R.J., *Forecasting. Methods and Applications*, 3rd edition, New York: Wiley & Sons, 1998.

[27] Ljung, M.G. & Box, G.E.P., On a measure of lack of fit in time series model. *Biometrika*, **65**, pp. 297–303, 1978.

[28] Jarque, C.M. & Bera, A.K., Model specification tests: A simultaneous approach. *Journal of Econometrics*, **20(1, A)**, pp. 59–82, 1982.

[29] Bhat, C.R., A heteroscedastic extreme value model of intercity travel mode choice. *Transportation Research*, **29B(6)**, pp. 471–483, 1997.

[30] Bhat, C.R., Covariance heterogeneity in nested logit models: Econometric structure and application to intercity travel. *Transportation Research*, **31B(1)**, pp. 11–21, 1997.

[31] Kroes, E., Lierens, A. & Kouwenhoven, M., The airport network and catchment area competition model: A comprehensive airport demand forecasting system using a partially observed database. Proceedings of ERSA 2005.

[32] Postorino, M.N. & Versaci, M., A neuro-fuzzy approach to simulate the user mode choice behaviour in a travel decision framework. *International Journal of Modelling and Simulation*, **27(4)**, 2007.

[33] Sadek, A.W., Spring, G. & Smith, B.L., Towards more effective transportation applications of computational intelligence paradigms. *Transportation Research Record*, **1836**, pp. 57–63, 2003.

[34] Pribyl, O. & Goulias K.G., Application of adaptive neuro-fuzzy inference system to analysis of travel behaviour. *Transportation Research Record*, **1854**, pp. 180–188, 2003.

[35] IATA, Air/rail intermodality study, Brussels, 2003.

[36] IATA, Passenger and freight forecast publications 2005–2009, www.iata.org.

[37] Eurocontrol, STATFOR, Long-term forecast of air traffic (1006–2025) report, www.eurocontrol.int/statfor, 2003.

5

Theory and practice in modelling air travel choice behaviour

S. Hess
University of Leeds, UK

Abstract

There is growing interest in modelling the choices made by air travellers. However, these choices are complex and many studies do not do that complexity justice. In this chapter, we take another look at the different choices made by an air passenger for a single journey and discuss ways of modelling these processes. We make a number of recommendations for good practice and also highlight a number of issues that need to be dealt with by the analysts. Finally, we present an application making use of state-of-the-art modelling techniques in an air travel behaviour context.

1 Introduction

An increasing number of studies are looking at modelling air travel choice behaviour, mainly with the help of discrete choice models. Existing applications range from the choice of air as a mode of travel [1] to the choice of airport in multi-airport regions [2, 3, 4, 5, 6, 7], the choice of airline or fare classes [8, 9], and the choice of access mode [10, 11]. Some applications look jointly at multiple travel dimensions, for example the joint choice of airport and airline [12] or even the choice of an airport, airline and access mode triplet [13]. Finally, there is also an increasing reliance on advanced model structures available, used for example in the representation of random taste heterogeneity across travellers [6, 7, 14], or the multi-dimensional correlation between alternatives sharing sub-choices along some of the travel dimensions [15].

Despite the recent progress in the area, a lot of work remains to be done. Indeed, the choice processes undertaken by air travellers are arguably more complex than those taken with other modes. While authors are gradually acknowledging this in their work, and while the use of advanced model structures has allowed for more realism, many studies still make strong assumptions that unduly simplify the choice processes. Crucially, there is also still a general lack of understanding of the actual choice processes undertaken by air travellers, a fact that is not helped by the dynamic nature of the problem at hand, as witnessed for example with the advance of low-cost carriers.

This chapter aims to take an overview look at the modelling issues and makes some suggestions for good practice. We first give an overview of the choice processes undertaken by air travellers (Section 2). This is followed in Section 3 by a discussion setting targets for practical research in this area while also acknowledging certain simplifications that are necessary in such analyses. Section 4 is concerned with data issues, while Section 5 looks at the question of model structure. Finally, Section 6 presents an empirical example, and Section 7 provides a brief summary of the chapter.

2 Air travel choice behaviour

The choices made by an air passenger for a single journey are complex and involve decisions along a number of different dimensions, some of which are strongly interrelated. In simple terms, the choices made by an air traveller can be divided into three main subcategories, namely those at the origin side, those at the destination side and those concerning the actual air journey. It is the latter ones and to some extent the origin side decisions that have received the most attention in the existing literature.

At the origin side of an air journey, a passenger chooses a departure airport and also makes a number of choices relating to the ground level journey to this departure airport. In many ways, the destination side choices are the mirror image of those made at the origin side.

This leaves us with choices relating to the actual air journey. Here, the first choice is that of an airline operating a route to the chosen destination. While most passengers will travel on a single airline for the duration of their journey, there are some routings on which passengers will have to rely on a combination of airlines, a situation that has in recent years increased in complexity given that a large number of routes are now operated under *code share* agreements. The next level of choice is that of a routing, which looks first at the choice between direct and connecting flights, before, when choosing a connecting flight, looking at the choice between different routes in terms of the number of connections and the choice of connecting airports. The final dimension of choice for the actual air journey is that of timing, that is the choice of a departure time and a departure date.

The above discussion has already shown that air journeys involve decisions along a multitude of dimensions. What makes the analysis of these choices even more complicated are the complex interdependencies between the various dimensions of choice, both in terms of interactions as well as ordering of priorities. To illustrate the latter point, it should be obvious that, for most passengers, the choice of destination will influence the choice set in terms of airlines or departure airports. However, there may also be passengers where the decision to travel on a specific airline (e.g. low-cost airline) will determine the choice set of possible destinations. From this perspective, a simultaneous modelling approach is clearly preferable to a potentially misguided sequential approach.

Finally, it should be acknowledged that passengers actually also make a decision to use air in the first place, as opposed to travelling on a different mode. For most destinations, this choice is a direct result of distance, making all other modes either impractical or impossible. However, for a number of short-haul destinations, there is increasing competition with high speed rail, and the analysis of the choices in this context are an interesting area for further work. However, mainly due to data requirements, most applications looking at detailed air travel choice dimensions have to rely on the assumption that the choice of air as a mode of travel has been made at a higher level, prior to making choices relating to the actual air journey.

3   Guidance for good modelling practice and contrast with status quo

The above discussion has highlighted the complexity of the choice processes undertaken by air travellers. This section sets out some guidelines for good practice and contrasts them with the status quo in modelling work.

3.1   Guidelines

3.1.1   Recognize the multi-dimensional nature of the choice process
Air travellers make choices among a multitude of travel dimensions, and not recognizing this in practical work can potentially lead to biased results. As an example, let us look at the case of a study that looks solely at the choice of airport but not the choice of airline. If a traveller in this study has a strong allegiance to an airline flying from a smaller airport with low overall frequency, then a simple airport choice model will be confused by the fact that this passenger actually flies from an airport with lower frequency to the desired destination. From this point of view, it is important to work on the basis of frequencies specific to airport-airline pairings, and not airport-specific frequency, as has commonly been the case in existing work. The same reasoning applies to other combinations of choice dimensions. In practice, this issue can be addressed by dividing the multi-dimensional alternative into a combination of elementary alternatives, with a passenger simultaneously choosing one alternative along each dimension of choice.

3.1.2   Account for correlation along different choice dimensions
By understanding the multi-dimensional nature of the choice process, it becomes evident that some of the *combined* alternatives share the attributes of other alternatives along one or more of the choice dimensions (e.g. same airline, same access mode). This clearly creates correlation between alternatives, and in the likely case where not all characteristics are observed by the analyst, this will

result in correlated error terms. Here, it is important to account for this correlation, as described in Section 5.2.

3.1.3 Use highly disaggregate level-of-service data

Many existing studies have produced poor results partly as a result of using an insufficient level of disaggregation in the level-of-service data, often as an effect of using simplifications along a number of choice dimensions. While some aggregation is almost inevitable, the use of an excessive amount of aggregation can lead to biased results. This can for example arise in the case of studies making use of weekly (or even monthly) data instead of daily data, hence ignoring the often significant variations in level-of-service attributes between different days of the week, especially in terms of flight frequencies.

3.1.4 Account for differences in behaviour across travellers

As in most contexts, there are significant differences between individual air travellers in their sensitivities to attributes affecting their journey, for example air fares and departure times. As a result, it is crucial to take such taste heterogeneity into account at the modelling stage, an issue that is addressed in more detail in Section 5.3.

3.2   Limitations of practical research

Without exemption, existing studies of air travel choice behaviour use a number of simplifications of the choice processes, often due to data issues. These simplifications can be looked at in turn for each of the various dimensions of choice:

- The *choice of destination* and the actual *decision to travel* are not generally modelled, where a reservation applies for the latter in the case of SC surveys giving respondents the option *not to travel*. It is thus normally assumed that these decisions are taken at an upper level, prior to the air-journey specific choices.
- As already mentioned above, the same reasoning applies to the *decision to travel by air*. Here, it is thus important to acknowledge that the estimates obtained from such models relate to the part of the population that has decided to travel by air, and are not representative of the overall population.
- The majority of studies of air travel choice behaviour look solely at the choice of *departure airport* and ignore the choice of *arrival airport*, a simplification primarily resulting from data issue.
- Just as for the choice of airport, the analysis of *ground level decisions* is generally limited to the origin end, again primarily due to data reasons. Additionally, most studies are only able to look at the choice of main mode, ignoring the possibility of trip-chaining, as well as the choice of different routes. The effects of these restrictions are dependent on the geographical context.

- In RP models, *trip timing* cannot generally be modelled due to a relative lack of information on preferred departure time and flight availabilities. These issues do not apply in the case of SC models.
- The issue of *flight routing* is generally left untreated in RP studies, while in SC studies, this is often limited to a choice between direct and connecting flights.
- Given the major role that airline allegiance plays for some travellers, advanced studies increasingly model the *choice of airline* in addition to the choice of airport. However, combinations of airlines are generally not allowed in such models, and additional issues can arise in the case of code share flights.

4 Data issues

One of the main problems that need to be faced in the modelling of air travel choice behaviour is that of data quality. This is the topic of the present section, where the discussion is divided into two parts, looking first at RP data before turning our attention to SC data.

4.1 Revealed preference data

4.1.1 Availability and attributes of unchosen alternatives

With RP data, the main issue that needs to be faced is the relative lack of information on the choice set that the traveller was faced with. While detailed information is generally available on the chosen flight, this does not extend to unchosen alternatives. In fact, in many cases, it is not even just the attributes of these alternatives that are unknown, but also their availability to a given traveller at a given time. Generally, an assumption of availability is required, alongside significant aggregation of level of service attributes for the unchosen flight options. Similar problems also arise along other dimensions, such as the access journey related choices, where again information on the availability and attributes of unchosen modes is often not available.

4.1.2 Fare data

Air fares should naturally be expected to play a major role in air travel choice behaviour. Despite this, the majority of RP studies of air travel choice behaviour have struggled or been unable to retrieve meaningful marginal fare effects. This is almost certainly a direct effect of the poor quality of the fare data, characterized by a high level of aggregation. Indeed, it is in most studies only possible to obtain information on the average fare charged by a given airline on a specific route. This clearly involves a great deal of aggregation, as no distinction is made between the fares paid across different travellers (i.e. in terms of travel classes as well as booking classes). With the dynamic nature of air fares, the levels used in modelling thus often bear little or no resemblance to those actually faced in the choice set, with the unavoidable implication of poor modelling results. Even though some progress can be made with the help of bookings data, issues of aggregation do remain. In fact, it can be seen that, in RP studies, disaggregate choice data is used in conjunction with aggregate level-of-service data, for at least some of the attributes. While, for some characteristics, this may be acceptable, it does, as described above, create significant problems in the treatment of air fares, and flight availability by extension.

4.1.3 Frequent flier information
While it is well known that airline allegiance as a result of membership in frequent flier programmes plays an important role in air travel choice behaviour, such information is often not collected in passenger surveys. As a result, this potentially crucial influence on choice behaviour cannot usually be taken into account in RP case studies.

4.1.4 Influence of other attributes
While most applications generally only look at a limited set of attributes, such as access time, flight time, frequency and fare, various other factors, such as on-time performance and in-flight entertainment, conceivably also have an influence on travellers' choices. Often, information on such attributes is however not available, potentially significantly increasing the error terms in the models, although some effects may be captured in airline specific constants.

4.1.5 Survey design issues and inter-dataset compatibility
The main input into RP air travel behaviour studies comes in the form of data collected at departure airports, generally by airport operators or civil aviation authorities. The factors of interest in these questionnaires often differ from those relevant to a modelling analysis (e.g. the lack of information on frequent flier programme membership), with the obvious impacts this has on any analysis. Additionally, compatible sources of level-of-service data need to be found.

4.2   Stated choice data

Some of the problems discussed above in the context of RP data can be alleviated by making use of SC data collected on the basis of tailor-made surveys, designed specifically for the use in advanced modelling analyses. Here, the main advantage is the fact that complete and accurate information is available on all alternatives faced by the respondent. From this point of view, it should come as no surprise that studies making use of SC data have been much more successful in retrieving significant effects for factors such as air fares and airline allegiance [cf. 16, 17]. However, it is important to remember that the use of SC data does pose some philosophical problems, in terms of how the behaviour differs from that observed in RP data [see, 18]. Additionally, issues of survey complexity need to be addressed. To allow respondents to better relate to the presented choices, surveys now often include a real-world reference alternative in the choice set; this however poses some additional issues, as discussed recently by Hess [19]. Both RP and SC data have advantages in their own right, and to a large extent, the choice of the optimal approach depends on the issues to be investigated, as well as the quality of the level-of-service data in the RP context. An interesting approach in this context is to combine RP and SC data, as done by Algers and Beser [20], hence correcting for the bias inherent to models estimated on SC data. The problem in this case however is one of obtaining compatible RP and SC datasets.

5 Model structure

Probably the most important question to address at the modelling stage is the choice of a mathematical structure. Given the important differences across travellers both in terms of behaviour as well as choice context, the use of a disaggregate modelling approach is clearly preferable to an aggregate one, and here, discrete choice structures belonging to the class of random utility models (RUM) have established themselves as the preferred approach. For an in-depth discussion of these modelling structures, see Train [21]. Here, we look solely at two main issues of great relevance in the analysis of air travel behaviour, namely that of inter-alternative correlation in the error terms (Section 5.2) and that of taste heterogeneity (Section 5.3) across travellers. This is preceded by a brief introduction of some common notation.

5.1   Basic concepts

A discrete choice model looks at the choices made by a *decision maker n* amongst a set of mutually exclusive alternatives contained in a choice set C_n. Each alternative $i = 1, ..., I$ in the choice set has an associated utility $U_{i,n}$, which is specific to decision-maker n, due to variations in attributes of the individuals, as well as in the attributes of the alternative, as faced by different decision-makers. Under the assumption of *utility maximising behaviour*, respondent n will choose alternative i if and only if $U_{i,n} > U_{j,n} \forall j \neq i$, with $i, j \in C_n$.

The utility of an alternative is a function of its attributes and the tastes of a decision maker. Given inherent randomness in behaviour as well as data limitations, only part of the utility can be observed, such that we rewrite:

$$U_{i,n} = V_{i,n} + \varepsilon_{i,n}, \tag{1}$$

with $V_{i,n}$ and $\varepsilon_{i,n}$ giving the *observed* and *unobserved* parts of utility, respectively. Here, $V_{i,n}$ is defined as $f(\beta_n, x_{i,n})$, where $x_{i,n}$ represents a vector of measurable (to the researcher) attributes of alternative i as faced by decision-maker n,[1] and β_n is a vector of parameters representing the tastes of decision-maker n, which is to be estimated from the data.

Due to the presence of the unobserved utility term $\varepsilon_{i,n}$, the deterministic choice process now becomes probabilistic, leading to a RUM, with the alternative with the highest observed utility having the highest probability of being chosen, where the individual probabilities are given by:

$$P_n(i) = P(\varepsilon_{j,n} - \varepsilon_{i,n} < V_{i,n} - V_{j,n} \forall_j \neq i). \tag{2}$$

After noting that the mean of the unobserved utility terms can be added to the observed part of utility in the form of an alternative-specific constant (ASC), the vector $\varepsilon_n = \{\varepsilon_{1,n}, \ldots, \varepsilon_{I,n}\}$ is now defined to be a random vector with joint density $f(\varepsilon_n)$, zero mean and covariance matrix Σ. From this, we can rewrite (2) as follows:

$$P_n(i) = \int_{\varepsilon_n} I(\varepsilon_{j,n} - \varepsilon_{i,n} < V_{i,n} - V_{j,n} \forall_j \neq i) f(\varepsilon_n) d\varepsilon_n, \qquad (3)$$

where $I(\cdot)$ is the indicator function which equals 1 if the term inside brackets is true and 0 otherwise. Different assumptions on the distribution of the error terms lead to different forms for the choice probabilities, and the multi-dimensional integral in Equation (3) will only take a closed form for certain choices of distribution for ε_n. In the most basic model, the multinomial logit (MNL) model, the error terms are assumed to be distributed identically and independently (*iid*), with more advanced models allowing for complex interdependencies.

5.2   Correlation between alternatives

As mentioned in Section 3.1.2, it is clearly a major and probably unwarranted assumption to rule out the presence of heightened correlation in the unobserved utility terms along any of the choice dimensions. Indeed, it cannot generally be expected that any commonalities between two alternatives sharing a common component along one or more of the choice dimensions would need to be explained in the observed part of utility. This makes basic models that assume independence of error terms, such as MNL, inappropriate for such modelling purposes.

The typical departure from the MNL model in the context of air travel choice behaviour has been to make use nested logit (NL) models which form the most basic nesting structure within the generalized extreme value (GEV) family of models, introduced by McFadden [22]. This set of models are all based on the use of the extreme-value distribution and allow for various levels of correlation among the unobserved part of utility across alternatives. This is accomplished by dividing the choice set into nests of alternatives, with increased correlation, and thus higher cross-elasticities, between alternatives sharing a nest. Alternatives sharing a nest are more likely substitutes for each other. These structures are generally represented by an upside-down tree, with the root at the top, elementary alternatives at the bottom and composite alternatives, or nests, in between.

In a two level NL model, alternatives are grouped into mutually exclusive nests, where, for each nest, a structural (nesting) parameter is estimated that relates to the level of correlation in the error terms of alternatives sharing that nest. One example of such a structure is to nest the alternatives by airport, that is allowing for heightened correlation between alternatives sharing the same departure airport. This structure is illustrated in Figure 1, with K mutually exclusive nests, one for each airport, and where each nest has its own nesting parameter, λ_k, thus allowing for different correlation levels with different airports.

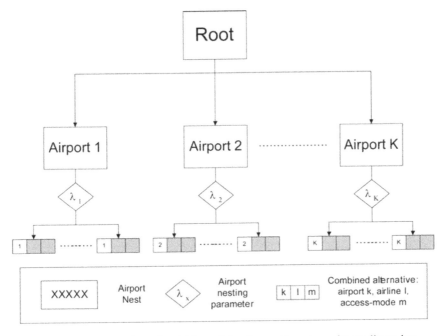

Figure 1: Structure of two-level NL model, using nesting along airport-dimension.

The example in Figure 1 can be replicated for the case of correlation along the airline dimension as well as correlation along the access mode dimension (or other dimensions of choice). However, the structure discussed so far only allow for correlation along one dimension of choice at a time. While it is possible to extend the NL structure to multiple dimensions of nesting, as shown in Figure 2 for the case of airport and airline choice,[2] where π_l is used as the nesting parameter for airline nests, this is not optimal. Indeed, the ordering of choice dimensions plays a role and the full level of correlation is only allowed for along the highest level of nesting. Indeed, by nesting the alternatives first by airport, and then by airline, the nest for airline l inside the nest for airport k will only group together the options on airline l for that airport k. The model is thus not able to capture correlation between alternatives using airline l at airport k_1 and alternatives using airline l at airport k_2, which is clearly a restriction. Finally, it can also be noted that this structure can only accommodate correlation along all but one of the dimensions of choice. Indeed, using the example shown in Figure 2, it can be seen that, by adding in an additional level of nesting by access mode below the airline level, each access mode nest would contain a single alternative, as the airline nest preceding the access mode nest would contain exactly one alternative for each access mode. As such, the lower level of nesting becomes obsolete.

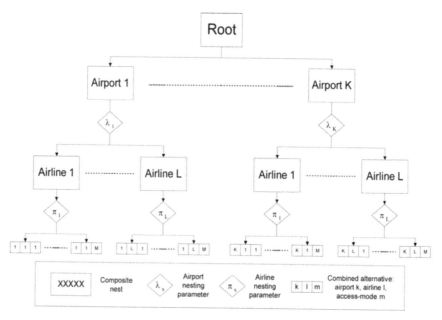

Figure 2: Structure of three-level NL model, using nesting along airport-dimension and airline-dimension.

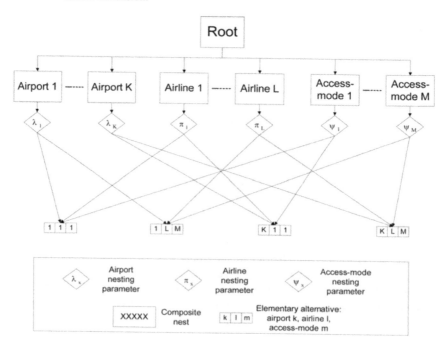

Figure 3: Structure of CNL model for the joint analysis of correlation along the airport, airline and access mode dimensions.

Both of these problems can be addressed by using a cross-nested logit (CNL) model, as discussed in the application in Section 6. This structure would be specified by defining three groups of nests, namely K airport nests, L airline nests and M access mode nests, and by allowing each alternative to belong to exactly one nest in each of these groups. The resulting structure allows for correlation along all three dimensions of choice and does so in a simultaneous rather than sequential fashion, that is not giving priority to one dimension of choice.

An example of such a model is shown in Figure 3, where, in addition to the previously defined λ_k and π_l, ψ_m is used as the structural parameter for access mode nest m. Again, only a subset of the composite nests and of the triplets of alternatives is shown. Additionally, the allocation parameters [cf. 21, Chapter 4], governing the proportion by which an alternative belongs to each of the three nests, are not shown in Figure 3.

5.3   Variation in behaviour across respondents

Another important issue that needs to be addressed during model specification are potential differences between travellers in their sensitivities to changes in attributes defining the alternatives. Such differences can clearly be seen to be likely to apply to air fare and travel sensitivities, but may also extend to other factors such as the willingness to pay for flying on a certain airline or on a certain type of aircraft. From this point of view, it is clearly a major assumption to make an assumption of taste homogeneity.

Various possible approaches exist to allow for taste heterogeneity. The most basic approach is to use discrete segmentations of the sample population, estimating separate models for different subsets of the sample, or in a less extreme case, separate coefficients within the same model. There are also many situations in which tastes can be expected to be related to socio-demographic attributes, such as lower cost sensitivity with rising income. While it would be possible to segment the sample population into different income classes, it may, in many cases, be preferable to allow for continuous interactions between tastes and sensitivities. Here, the modeller needs to additionally make a choice between linear or non-linear interactions.

Due to data limitations as well as inherent randomness in sensitivities, not all taste heterogeneity can be explained in a deterministic fashion, and analysts are increasingly turning to models such as mixed multinomial logit (MMNL) that allow for a representation of random (as opposed to deterministic) taste heterogeneity. In a MMNL model, the choice probabilities are given by integrals of MNL probabilities over the assumed distribution of taste coefficients. Although incredibly flexible, the MMNL model comes with a high computational cost due to the reliance on simulation in estimation and application.

The various methods for representing taste heterogeneity are characterized by differences in terms of flexibility, ease of implementation/estimation and ease of interpretation. These factors are strongly correlated, with more advanced specifications offering gains in flexibility at the expense of higher computational cost as well as issues in interpretation. Nevertheless, whichever approach is used, it is important to at least challenge the assumption of taste homogeneity.

5.4 Discussion

The modelling approaches described in Section 5.2 and Section 5.3 have quite separate aims; the analysis of inter-alternative correlation, along multiple dimensions, and the representation of deterministic and random variations in choice behaviour. When both phenomena play a role simultaneously, analysts may need to rely on even more advanced model structures that allow for the joint representation of inter-alternative correlation and random taste heterogeneity [cf. 23, 24].

6 Empirical example

For the empirical example used in this section, we summarize part of the results described in the study by Hess and Polak [15]. Particularly, we look at the combined choice of airport, airline and access mode for air passengers departing from Greater London.

6.1 Description of data

The application described here made use of RP data, with information on actual trips taken from the 1996 passenger survey conducted by the Civil Aviation Authority [25]. The final sample used for the analysis reported here contained data from 8704 respondents travelling for business reasons with the London departure being the outbound leg of the journey. A total of 31 destinations used in the analysis, all served by a single airport, and spread across Great Britain, Europe, the Middle East and North America. For short haul destinations an assumption was made that respondents made an a priori assumption to travel by air. Air-side level-of-service data were obtained from BACK aviation, with information on fares compiled from the International Passenger Survey [26] and the fare supplement of the Official Airways Guide for 1996 [27]. As is the case with most RP studies, the resulting dataset is of highly aggregate nature, leading to the previously discussed problems in the estimation of the marginal utility of air fares (cf. Section 4.1.2). Additionally, no information was available on frequent flier programmes. Finally, for the analysis of the ground-level choice dimension, data from the national airport access model (NAAM) were obtained for the base year 1999 [28], and corresponding cost information for 1996 was produced with the help of the retail price index, while assuming that relative travel times have on average stayed constant.

6.2 Model structure and specification

The final choice contained five departure airports, namely Heathrow (LHR), Gatwick (LGW), Stansted (STN), Luton (LTN) and London City (LCY). This mix of major airports, outlying airports and a small city centre airport means the area if of special interest in the context of the present book. Along the airline dimension, there were 37 options, airlines, with six modes available along the access journey dimension.[3] This leads to a total of 1110 combinations of airports, airlines and access modes arise. However, with not all airlines operating from all airports, the total number of airport–airline pairs is actually 54, which reduces the number of alternatives (airport, airline, access mode triplets) to 324.[4]

A large number of different attributes were used in the initial modelling analysis, including attributes relating to the air journey, such as frequency, fare, flight time, aircraft type and seat capacity, and attributes relating to the access journey, such as access cost, in-vehicle access time (IVT), out-of-vehicle access time, wait time, number of interchanges and parking cost. Different model structures were investigated, namely MNL, two-level NL and CNL, where in all models, weights were used in the specification of the log-likelihood function to account for the quota used in data collection, which are not representative of the population level.

6.3 Model results

Despite an extensive specification search, only a limited number of attributes were observed to have a significant impact on behaviour, namely access cost, IVT, flight frequency and flight time, where a log-transform was used for all four attributes. Crucially, no effect could be identified for air fare, where this is at least partly due to the poor quality of the data as discussed in Section 4.1.2. The list of significant attributes was observed to stay identical across model structures, i.e. MNL, NL and CNL.

Table 1 presents a summary of the mathematical performance of the different models. Here we can see that all three NL models outperform the MNL model, with the best performance offered by the model using nesting by access mode. In turn, the CNL model outperforms not only MNL but also all three NL structures. Finally, the total improvement of the CNL model over the MNL model is bigger than the combined improvements in the adjusted ρ^2 measure for the three NL models. However, while the results show that the CNL model offers significant improvements over the more simple NL models, these come at the expense of a very significant increase in estimation cost.

Table 1: Model performance on London data.

Model	Final LL	Parameters	Adjusted ρ^2
MNL	−14,945.3	55	0.3445
NL by airport	−14,896.1	59	0.3465
NL by airline	−14,870.7	74	0.3469
NL by access mode	−14,816.7	60	0.3499
CNL	−14,603.9	91	0.3578

Table 2: Model results for London data.

	IVT vs. access cost	Freq. vs. access cost	Freq. vs. IVT	Flight time vs. IVT
	(£/hour)	(£/flight)	(hours/flight)	
MNL				
Minimum	1.18	0.02	0.01	0.04
Mean	16.24	1.56	0.11	1.07
Maximum	143.38	231.05	4.06	7.43
Standard deviation	25.44	4.85	0.18	0.7
NL by airport				
Minimum	1.3	0.02	0.01	0.04
Mean	17.85	1.63	0.11	0.97
Maximum	157.65	242.38	3.87	6.72
Standard deviation	27.98	5.09	0.17	0.63
NL by airline				
Minimum	1.29	0.03	0.01	0.04
Mean	17.76	1.79	0.12	1.13
Maximum	156.8	265.11	4.26	7.85
Standard deviation	27.83	5.57	0.19	0.74
NL by access mode				
Minimum	0.99	0.02	0.01	0.04
Mean	13.52	1.11	0.1	1.05
Maximum	119.35	164.74	3.47	7.31
Standard deviation	21.18	3.46	0.15	0.69
CNL				
Minimum	1.16	0.01	0	0.04
Mean	15.96	0.9	0.07	0.95
Maximum	140.89	132.96	2.38	6.59
Standard deviation	25	2.79	0.1	0.62

We next turn our attention to substantive results, which are summarized in Table 2. Given the use of the log-transform in nominators as well as denominators, the various trade-offs were calculated separately for each individual,[5] and summary statistics were then calculated across respondents. We can see that the first three models produce roughly similar results, while those produced by the CNL model and the NL model using nesting access mode are more extreme (when compared to the three first models), especially when looking at the value of travel time savings (VTTS) measures for the model using nesting by access mode.

Another observation that can be made for the trade-offs is that the VTTS measures are markedly lower than those reported, for example, by Pels *et al.* [3], although they are still higher than in other contexts, which can be explained partly by concepts of risk-averseness, as discussed, for example, by Hess and Polak [7]. Travellers are willing to pay for a reduction in the risk of missing their flight, where this risk clearly increases with access time. The still high values should also be put into context by noting that the average access journey in this population segment was measured as 57 minutes.

Finally, a detailed analysis of the correlation structure in the different models [cf. 15] highlights the presence of high levels of correlation between the errors for alternatives sharing the same airport, airline or access mode. Here, the CNL model was more successful at retrieving these correlation patterns than was the case for the different NL structures.

7 Summary and conclusions

The discussion in this chapter has highlighted the complexity of the choice processes undertaken by air travellers, with decisions being taken along a multitude of dimensions. In practice however, it is almost inevitable to use some simplifications of the choice process, partly because of modelling complexity, but mainly because of data issues. In this context, the *advantages* of SC data make the use of such datasets an important avenue for further research, potentially in conjunction with compatible RP data.

The problems that need to be faced when making use of RP data were also highlighted in the empirical example in Section 6 where it was not possible to retrieve significant effects for a range of important variables that included air fares, schedule delay, and airline and airport allegiance. From a model structure point of view, the application has shown that the use of more advanced model structures can lead to improvements in model fit. However, although the improvements are statistically significant, they are too small to lead to any major differences in model performance. Nevertheless, the advanced model structures provide further insights into choice behaviour, and there are also differences in the substantive results between the various models.

The one common observation from this application and that of other studies is that the results do suggest that access time plays a major role in the choice process, with passengers having a strong preference for their local airport. As such, the attractiveness of outlying airports depends heavily on good access connections, unless there are other incentives, such as low air fares. This is reflected in the fact that only low-cost carriers find it relatively easy to attract passengers to outlying airports that are not served by convenient and fast ground-level services. It is conceivable that the sensitivity to access time decreases with flight time [cf. 17], such that moving long haul services to outlying airports would seem wise; this however causes problems as the associated (and necessary) short haul feeder flights will also carry point-to-point passengers, who will again have a preference for more centrally-located airports.

Acknowledgements

The author would like to acknowledge the input of John Polak in earlier stages of this work and would similarly like to thank the Civil Aviation Authority and the Department for Transport for data support.

Notes

1. The vector $x_{i,n}$ potentially also includes interactions with socio-demographic attributes of respondent n.
2. It is important to stress that this should not be seen as representing a sequential choice process. Rather, it means that there is correlation between two alternatives that share the same airport, but that the correlation is larger if they additionally share the same airline.
3. The options were private car, rental car, public transport (rail, bus, local transport), long distance coach, taxi and minicab (MC), where, for data reasons, no combinations of modes were considered in the present analysis.
4. The number of available alternatives for specific individuals in the estimation sample ranges from 6 to 58, with a mean of 31.
5. With $U = \ldots + \beta_1 \ln(x_1) + \beta_2 \ln(x_2) + \ldots$, the ratio of the partial derivatives of U with respect to x_1 and x_2 is given by $\beta_1/\beta_2 \, x_2/x_1$, as opposed to the simple β_1/β_2 ratio used in the case of a linear parameterization.

References

[1] González-Savignat, M., Competition in air transport: The case of high speed train. *Journal of Transport Economics and Policy*, **38(1)**, 77–108, 2004.
[2] Pels, E., Nijkamp, P. & Rietveld, P., Airport and airline choice in a multi-airport region: An empirical analysis for the San Francisco bay area. *Regional Studies*, **35(1)**, pp. 1–9, 2001.
[3] Pels, E., Nijkamp, P. & Rietveld, P., Access to and competition between airports: A case study for the San Francisco Bay area. *Transportation Research Part A: Policy and Practice*, **37(1)**, pp. 71–83, 2003.
[4] Pathomsiri, S., Mahmassani, H. & Haghani, A., *Airport Choice Model for Baltimore-Washington Region*. Paper presented at the 83rd annual meeting of the Transportation Research Board, Washington, DC, 2004.
[5] Basar G. & Bhat, C.R., A parameterized consideration set model for airport choice: An application to the San Francisco Bay area. *Transportation Research Part B: Methodological*, **38(10)**, pp. 889–904, 2004.
[6] Hess S. & Polak, J.W., Accounting for random taste heterogeneity in airport-choice modelling. *Transportation Research Record*, **1915**, pp. 36–43, 2005.
[7] Hess, S. & Polak, J.W., Mixed logit modelling of airport choice in multi-airport regions. *Journal of Air Transport Management*, **11(2)**, pp. 59–68, 2005.
[8] Proussaloglou, K. & Koppelman, F.S., Air carrier demand: An analysis of market share determinants. *Transportation*, **22(4)**, pp. 371–388, 1995.

[9] Chin, A.T.H. Impact of frequent flyer programs on the demand for air travel. *Journal of Air Transportation*, **7(2)**, pp. 53–86, 2002.

[10] Monteiro, A.B.F. & Hansen, M., Improvements to airport ground access and behavior of multiple airport system: BART extension to San Francisco International Airport. *Transportation Research Record*, **1562**, pp. 38–47, 1997.

[11] Psaraki, V. & Abacoumkin, C., Access mode choice for relocated airports: The new Athens International Airport. *Journal of Air Transport Management*, **8(2)**, pp. 89–98, 2002.

[12] Bondzio, L., Modelle für den Zugang von Passagieren zu Flughäfen (Models for the Passengers' Access to Airports), PhD thesis, Ruhr-University, Bochum, 1996.

[13] Hess, S. & Polak, J.W., Airport, airline and access mode choice in the san francisco bay area. *Papers in Regional Science*, **85(4)**, pp. 543–567, 2006.

[14] Hess, S., Posterior analysis of random taste coefficients in air travel choice behaviour modelling. *Journal of Air Transport Management*, **13(4)**, pp. 203–212, 2007.

[15] Hess, S. & Polak, J.W., Exploring the potential for cross-nesting structures in airport-choice analysis: A case-study of the Greater London area. *Transportation Research Part E: Logistics and Transportation Review*, **42(2)**, pp. 63–81, 2006.

[16] Adler, T., Falzarano, C.S. & Spitz, G., *Modeling Service Trade-offs in Air Itinerary Choices*. Paper presented at the 84th annual meeting of the Transportation Research Board, Washington, DC, 2005.

[17] Hess, S., Adler, T. & Polak, J.W., Modelling airport and airline choice behavior with stated-preference survey data. *Transportation Research Part E: Logistics and Transportation Review*, **43**, pp. 221–233, 2007.

[18] Louviere, J.J., Hensher, D.A. & Swait, J., *Stated Choice Models: Analysis and Application*, Cambridge: Cambridge University Press, 2000.

[19] Hess, S., Treatment of reference alternatives in stated choice surveys for air travel choice behaviour. *Journal of Air Transport Management*, **14(5)**, pp. 275–279, 2008.

[20] Algers, S. & Beser, M., Modelling choice of flight and booking class: A study using stated preference and revealed preference data. *International Journal of Services Technology and Management*, **2(1–2)**, pp. 28–45, 2001.

[21] Train, K., *Discrete Choice Methods with Simulation*, Cambridge, MA: Cambridge University Press, 2003.

[22] McFadden, D., Modelling the choice of residential location (Chapter 25). *Spatial Interaction Theory and Planning Models*, eds. A. Karlqvist, L. Lundqvist, F. Snickars & J. W. Weibull, Amsterdam: North Holland, pp. 75–96, 1978.

[23] Walker, J., Extended Discrete Choice Models: Integrated Framework, Flexible Error Structures, and Latent Variables, PhD thesis, MIT, Cambridge, MA, 2001.

[24] Hess, S., Bierlaire, M. & Polak, J.W., Capturing taste heterogeneity and correlation structure with Mixed GEV models (Chapter 4). *Applications*

of Simulation Methods in Environmental and Resource Economics, eds. R. Scarpa & A. Alberini, Dordrecht, The Netherlands: Springer, pp. 55–76, 2005.

[25] Civil Aviation Authority (CAA), UK airports Passenger survey, CAP 677: Passengers at Birmingham, Gatwick, Heathrow, London City, Luton, Manchester and Stansted in 1996, The Civil Aviation Authority, London, 1996.

[26] ONS, *International Passenger Survey*, London: The Office for National Statistics, 1996.

[27] OAG, *World Airways Guide Fares Supplement 1996*, Dunstable, UK: Reed Elsevier, 1996.

[28] Scott Wilson Kirkpatrick, *National Airport Accessibility Model: Model Status Report* (Prepared for the Department for Transport), Basingstoke: Scott Wilson Kirkpatrick & Co Ltd., 1999.

6

Practical airport demand forecasting with capacity constraint: methodology and application

E. P. Kroes
Den Haag and VU University of Amsterdam, The Netherlands

Abstract

Airports require demand forecasts for operational, tactical and strategic purposes. This chapter provides a description of a practical, operational methodology that has been developed to provide such demand forecasts, for horizons ranging from short term (next year) to long term (20 years ahead or more); and for regional airports as well as major international airports. The model system consists of three elements: a demand model, a supply model and an iterative procedure to take account of capacity constraints. The demand model uses three main components: a detailed data base describing existing passenger flows between air zones worldwide, a growth model describing expected relative increases in passenger flows and a discrete choice based competition model allocating passenger flows to different airports, airlines, air routes and alternative modes of transport. The supply model is essentially a three-dimensional cross-table of aircraft movements, distinguishing movements by size, technology class and time-of-day of departure. Starting from a detailed data base of existing aircraft movements, a simple aging method combined with incremental log-linear modelling provides estimates of future aircraft movements. A shadow-price mechanism is used to adjust demand and supply levels to fit within the limits of available runway and environmental capacity, if necessary. We have also described two applications of the methodology to Amsterdam Airport, one addressing long-term airport capacity issues and the other exploring the expected impact of an air flight tax for the Netherlands.

Keywords: air demand forecasting; airport competition; airport capacity constraint; time-series models; random utility models.

1 Introduction

A few decades ago air transport analysts have been using trend extrapolation (a simple form of time-series analysis) to obtain estimates of demand in the near future. Since then more advanced methods of time-series analysis have been applied, using causal factors such as economic development, as the key drivers of growth. The implicit assumption was still that the market shares of the airports under consideration would remain constant, even in the longer term. Such an assumption might be justified in a largely regulated environment.

However, in more recent years new dynamics and constraints have entered the system. Liberalization has led to more competition between airlines and airports. This dramatically increased competition between airports, airlines and alliances on the one hand, and led to serious airport capacity issues on the other, which made extrapolations of historic demand no longer adequate. Airport demand forecasts now need to take account of the many competitive elements and the physical and environmental constraints in addition to standard growth scenarios.

As a consequence discrete choice models have found there way to explain how choices of (potential) air passengers, reacting to a multitude of competing offers, affect airport traffic flows. Chapter 4 has given an overview of the various demand forecasting methods, while Chapter 5 has given an extensive description of the most advanced methods of airport choice modelling.

In this chapter, we have a somewhat more practical focus: here we describe how we use a combination of the different available methods to arrive at estimates of expected future passenger volumes for airports, whether regional or main airport. In order to do that we represent decisions by potential air passengers (the demand side: passenger numbers) and airlines (the supply side: aircraft movements) and their interaction, subject to external capacity constraints (physical, environmental); in other words an equilibrium model approach.

In this paper, we provide a brief description of the AEOLUS model and its main components. Then we report two applications of the model for Amsterdam airport: first to assess capacity issues and a range of policy measures for the planning horizons 2020 and 2040, and second to estimate the short and medium term impact of alternative flight tax measures in the Netherlands.

2 Approach

The formal objective of the air demand forecasting model described here was to develop a practical, operational tool capable of providing air demand forecasts at airport level, for planning and policy evaluation purposes. In addition to this fairly general objective a large number of requirements were specified, including the following (in random order):

- the model had to be strategic in nature and suitable for quick policy evaluation;
- the model had to be reasonably quick in terms of computing time and pragmatic in application;

- the methodology had to be intuitive and transparent in its operation;
- the model had to take into account the competition between airports and airlines (including low-cost airlines and alliances) in North-West Europe;
- it had to take into account the landside accessibility of the airports under consideration;
- the model had to include competition with surface transport modes including high-speed rail where relevant;
- it had to take into account the effects of both airport capacity and noise constraints;
- the method should be suitable for assessing the implications of a range of policy measures (such as levies for specific market segments);
- the methodology should be capable of assessing the welfare effects of the capacity constraints and policy measures.

The combination of the objective and the many requirements has lead to a fairly simple modelling approach; it would have been impossible to include for instance state-of-the-art demand modelling techniques as described in Chapter 4 in the system, as the run-times would have become excessive. On the other hand the model system is unusually comprehensive, in that it includes also explicit supply-side modelling, and pragmatic, in that it uses whatever data is available and generates the missing detail where necessary.

The model considers worldwide traffic flows to, from and through the airports under consideration. The architecture of the simulation system consists of two modules: a module to forecast traveller choices (e.g. which airports to depart from? Which air route?) and a module to forecast airline choices (which mix of aircraft to use?). The traveller choice module requires current passenger counts and level-of-service data for calculating travellers' preferences for the available alternatives in the current base year (in this example 2003). The airline choice module computes numbers of yearly flights per type of aircraft and per period of the day, also for the base year (in this example 2003; see Figure 1).

The observed numbers of passengers in the base year are extrapolated towards the forecast year (for instance 2020, in the example) using origin-destination (OD) specific growth factors that depend on expected economic and price developments between each OD pair. This is essentially a simple time-series model.

The distribution over departure airports, air routes etc. is calculated again in the travellers' choice module, this time using the level-of-service anticipated for the forecast year. And the airline choice module is also calculated for the forecast year. The traveller choice module is connected to the airline choice module by an iterative loop, to meet any capacity constraints that may arise in the forecast year.

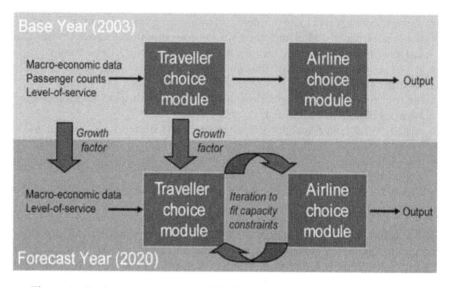

Figure 1: Basic structure of the AEOLUS model.

3 Demand forecasts

The demand forecasting method within the AEOLUS model contains three elements:

1. An observed base year passenger flow data base.
2. A growth factor model.
3. A traveller choice module.

The logic is as follows:

1. Starting point is the existing observed base year pattern of passenger flows: the numbers of passengers travelling from each origin to each destination through all airports and modes. No attempt is made to model this base year situation, to explain the frequency of air travel or the OD pattern (distribution). By working this way the model is by definition consistent with the base year statistics, and the complex interactions that exist within the base year demand profile are retained without explicitly trying to capture them.
2. Growth factors are then used to extrapolate the base year OD pattern to new year t volumes. This is done by using demand elasticities for key drivers of air travel volume, such as GDP. The elasticities are applied using OD specific developments in the drivers, and separately for different journey purposes. By combining 1 and 2 a new modified OD matrix is obtained for the target year.
3. The traveller choice module reproduces the decisions of the air passengers, and in particular how those affect the market shares of different airports under consideration. The module is applied both for the base year and for the forecast horizon, to obtain a factor that indicates the increase or decrease in market share. This module simulates the expected change in competitive

position of the airports under consideration, as a function of changes in the air network (destinations, frequencies, alliances, hub-structure), air fares and also surface accessibility.

All three elements are used in combination to obtain the ultimate demand forecasts:

$$V_{ijp}^{t} = V_{ijp}^{b} \operatorname{Fac}_{ijp}^{t} \left(P_{ijp}^{ta} / P_{ijp}^{ba} \right),$$

where: V_{ijp}^{t} = volume of air passengers in year t;

   i = origin zone;

   j = destination zone;

   p = purpose;

   V_{ijp}^{b} = volume of air passengers in base year b;

   $\operatorname{Fac}_{ijp}^{t}$ = growth factor of passenger volume from year b to year t;

   P_{ijp}^{ta} = proportion of air passengers using airport a in year t;

   P_{ijp}^{ba} = proportion of air passengers using airport a in base year b.

Each of these elements is described in some more detail in the subsequent sections.

3.1 Traveller choice module

The traveller choice module simulates the number of long-distance trips that travellers make between all airports worldwide, which are represented in origin and destination zones. And in particular, it calculates how these trips are distributed over the wide range of available choice alternatives.

The total number of zones worldwide is typically some 100, with the geographic coverage of the origin and destination zones being relatively small within the catchment area of airport(s) under investigation. The zones become larger for destinations within the same continent when distances to the airport increase, and the zones are very large for intercontinental trips.

For trips with an origin (or destination) within the catchment area of the airport(s) under consideration, the model forecasts the market shares for each of the possible departure (or arrival) airports in this region (see Figure 2 for an example of the airports in the catchment area of Amsterdam airport) and the market shares of the modes used to access (or egress from) the airport. For trips with an origin (or destination) inside the catchment area of the airport and with a destination (or origin) somewhere else on the same continent, the model forecasts the distribution over the available main modes as well: car, train (high-speed) and aircraft. This specific structure reflects air passenger choices among competing departure and hub airports in north-west Europe in a straightforward way.

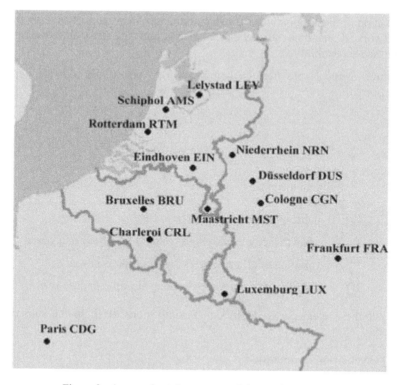

Figure 2: Assumed catchment area of Amsterdam airport.

The market shares of the available combinations of travel alternatives are determined by simulating traveller choices at up to three levels (see Figure 3):

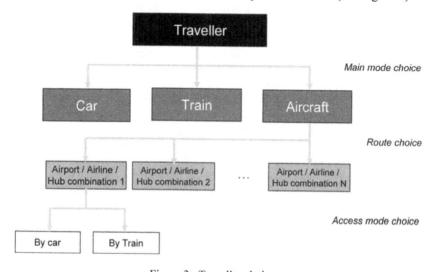

Figure 3: Traveller choices.

1. The choice between main modes of transport from O to D: car, train (high-speed) or aircraft.
2. The choice between available air routes, specified by departure airport, airline or alliance, direct flight or indirect flight via a hub.
3. The choice between access modes to the airport: normally car or train.

Not all choices are modelled for each OD combination, see Table 1.

Table 1: Choices that are modelled for each origin–destination combination.

Origin	Destination		
	Catchment area	*Rest of Europe*	*Rest of world*
Catchment area	(Out of scope)	Main mode choice; Route choice; Access mode choice	Route choice; Access mode choice
Rest of Europe	Main mode choice; Route choice; Egress mode choice	Route choice	Route choice
Rest of world	Route choice; Egress mode choice	Route choice	Route choice

The AEOLUS model uses random utility models, in this case standard nested logit [1], to simulate the traveller choices. Travel times, waiting and transfer times, travel costs, and service frequencies are the main determinants of choice included in the utility functions. The coefficients have been inferred from a number of previous studies, and a large number of alternative-specific constants are calibrated from base year air passenger statistics for airports in the catchment area.

3.1.1 Access mode choice

Two alternatives are typically included here: car and train (if available, or coach). Generalized costs for the car mode are determined by fuel cost, parking cost and travel time. Travel times are converted into generalized cost by means of multiplication by a value-of-time depending on the travel purpose (business or non-business). Generalized costs for the train mode are determined by the train fare and generalized train travel time. Travel fares and times are taken from an input file with surface access level-of-service information for all departure airports in the area under consideration.

The same model is used to model the egress mode in case the destination of the trip is within the catchment area (backward journey).

3.1.2 Route choice

The choice alternatives are defined by airline (e.g. Skyteam, Star Alliance, OneWorld, low-cost airlines, other airlines), by hub (direct flight, or one of the

64 international hubs considered) and by access/egress airport (only if origin or destination is within the catchment area). The utility of each alternative is determined by the logarithm of the number of flights per week, by a generalized cost term (determined by an assumed ticket fare and flight time (with an extra penalty for an indirect flight)) and by an accessibility term for the airport (only in catchment area). This accessibility term is the *logsum* of the access mode choice model. Air level of service information including destinations served, flight frequencies, fares, flight times, interconnections, etc. are taken from an input file. This has been prepared using Official Airline Guide (OAG) [2] flight data and a fares model.

3.1.3 Main mode choice
There are three choice alternatives here: car, train (high-speed) and aircraft. The utilities for the first two modes are determined by travel cost (fuel or train fare) and generalized travel time; the utility of the air alternative is determined by the *logsum* of the route choice model. Level of service for car and (high-speed) rail is obtained from international surface transport network data.

3.1.4 Air Freight model
In addition to the passenger demand model, a small air freight demand model can also be used. In this model both the volume of air freight and its distribution among alternative airlines and full freighters and belly-freight can be simulated.

3.2 Observed base year OD matrix

Another key component of the demand model system is the observed base year pattern of air trips. This is derived from a combination of different sources:

- passenger surveys on airports (e.g. the 'continuous survey' carried out at Amsterdam airport);
- detailed passenger statistics (annual volumes by destination) published by airports;
- other international sources of information on surface transport.

In the ideal case complete and accurate information for all OD flows should be available, for all airports, airlines/alliances, air routes, surface transport modes, etc. In practice this is often not available, or only in the form of aggregate information. Our pragmatic solution for this has been that we have used detailed passenger survey data for a single airport in combination with the traveller choice model described above, to estimate the missing OD information for the other airports.

In short the procedure works as follows. The unobserved volume for an airport k is calculated by multiplying the observed volume l by the ratio between the simulated market share of alternative k and l:

$$V_{unobserved}(k) = (\text{Market share}(k)/\text{Markets share}(l))V_{observed}(l).$$

If the simulated market shares for airport l are not too close to 0 this generally gives credible results. This method is described in some more detail in [3].

In practice, obtaining a reasonable accurate 'observed' base year OD matrix is often a substantial activity, which requires a major effort. And the result will inevitably be subject to some error. But when one makes sure that all available information is taken into account, that at least a fairly accurate source of OD information for one important airport is included, and that the marginal distributions for all airports are checked against the published statistics (and corrected where necessary), this forms a reasonable starting point for the modelling procedure.

3.3 Growth factor model

The growth factor model provides factors which are applied to the observed base year passenger volumes to obtain the future year OD matrix. The specification is simple:

$$\text{Fac}_{ijp}^{t} = \left(\text{Driver}_{dijp}^{t} / \text{Driver}_{dijp}^{b} \right) \text{Elast}_{ijp},$$

where: Elast_{ijp} = Demand elasticity for Driver d, OD pair i-j and purpose p;
Driver_{dijp}^{t} = Driver of demand growth d, OD pair i-j and purpose p.

This procedure is applied on a year-by-year basis, for as many years as are necessary. We use the following drivers of growth:

- population size for purpose leisure;
- GDP for purpose leisure;
- trade volume for purpose business;
- price for purposes leisure and business.

For OD relations, we take the average of the drivers' values for origin and destination zone.

Because the values of driver growth are often different for different OD pairs (e.g. expected future GDP growth for Asian zones is much higher than for European zones) the structure of the OD matrix is modified by the application of this growth-factor procedure.

4 Supply forecasts

Often a substantial growth of air traffic is predicted. The resulting numbers of aircraft movements in the coming 10 to 20 years often exceed the current runway capacity. Furthermore, the amount of noise generated by aircraft may exceed existing legal boundaries. And the same may hold for other environmental emissions. To take these effects into account, we developed an airline choice module that simulates the deployment of a mix of different aircraft to transport the passenger volume as predicted by the traveller module. This module distinguishes three dimensions:

1. the size of the aircraft (nine classes);
2. the technological status of the aircraft (five classes);
3. the time-period of departure/arrival (four periods per day).

This results in 180 possible combinations.

We have used observed base year distributions, and foreseeable trends to predict the future distribution of aircraft over these 180 combinations. One such foreseeable trend is the future renewal of the aircraft fleet, based upon a simple aging model. From this distribution, we infer the implicit preference utility values for each of the combinations (the table is seen as a log-linear model, where each cell has an associated utility which can be inferred from its share). When for instance airport charges are introduced, these utilities are modified (costs per seat are computed and converted into utility values, and added to the base utility using an assumed cost coefficient). This type of application is similar to the well-known incremental logit-modelling approach, described for instance in [1]. After modification of the utilities new shares can be computed, and new distributions over the possible combinations can be determined (Figure 4). This enables us to simulate how autonomous developments (through aging of the fleet), capacity constraints (through shadow cost) or policies (through actual cost increases) modify the distributions of aircraft used.

An estimate of the total number of aircraft movements (per year and per period of the day) and the total environmental burden (i.e. the amount of noise generated by the departing and arriving aircraft) can be calculated using this airline choice model.

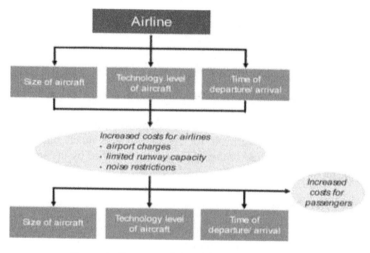

Figure 4: Structure of the airline choices module.

4.1 Forecasting demand and supply

For the base year the passenger choice and the airline choice module are run once to calculate a base scenario. The output values for the number of passengers, the number of flights and the volume of noise produced are calibrated using correction factors to match the observed values in the base year. Typically only small corrections are necessary.

For the forecast year we specify:

- the expected changes in air level-of-service (increase of flight frequencies, change in air fares, flight times typically remain constant);
- the expected changes in level-of-service of the land modes (fuel cost, train fares, travel times);
- the expected change in value-of-time (due to real increase of incomes);
- the expected changes in the airlines' preferences for the deployment of aircrafts of certain sizes (due to the availability of larger aircraft);
- the expected changes in the airlines' preferences for the deployment of aircrafts of certain technology (due to the availability of newer and more quite aircraft). For this we use a simple fleet aging and replacement model.

The number of travellers in the forecast year travelling between an origin and a destination zone are determined by applying a growth factor to the number of travellers in the base year. For non-business travellers this growth factor depends on population growth in the origin zone, real GDP per capita growth in the origin zone and the price growth in both origin and destination zones. For business travellers, this growth factor depends on trade growth between the origin and destination zone and price growth. Price elasticities are within the ranges indicated by Brons *et al.* [4].

The passenger choice module is then run again to determine the market shares of the available alternatives in the forecast year. Consecutively, the airline choice module is run again to calculate the number of aircraft movements and the amount of generated noise in the forecast year.

5 Capacity constraint

If demand in the forecast year exceeds supply, during any of the time periods considered, a capacity constraint procedure is necessary in order to establish a consistent equilibrium solution. In the model system this works as follows. If the total number of aircraft movements exceeds either the physical (runway) capacity or the legal environmental noise limit, an iterative procedure is started (Figure 5). In each iteration the passenger airfares are increased by a shadow cost, so that demand is reduced and airlines that fly with larger aircraft and/or from airports with less severe capacity constraints become relatively more attractive. In parallel, charges for the airlines stimulate the use of larger and more modern (i.e. less noisy) aircraft. This iterative procedure is repeated until the demand (passengers converted into aircraft movements) can be accommodated within the capacity limits.

The user of the AEOLUS model can choose between two options for the way the shadow costs are allocated: slot allocation based upon slot trading, or a system based on grandfathering rights. The first option allocates a charge to each aircraft movement, independent of the airline. Since these costs are partly transferred to the passengers by increased air fares, the final distribution of slots will favour those airlines (and those passengers) that have the highest willingness to pay for such a slot. This simulates a free slot trading system where airlines may win and loose slots.

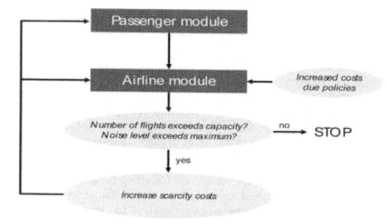

Figure 5: Iterative procedure.

The second option keeps the number of flights per airline in the base year fixed. This means that slots that have been allocated to an airline in the past, can not be transferred to another airline (this is called the system of grandfathering rights). Any remaining slots that have not been allocated in the base year are distributed over the airlines proportional to their demand for additional slots. However, a small number of slots are given to the smaller airlines to simulate the current policy to stimulate new entrants in the market.

In case of slot trading, the shadow cost is (partly) dependent on the amount of noise that an aircraft generates in case the noise limitations are exceeded. This stimulates the choice for newer types of aircraft. In case of a slot allocation system with grandfathering rights there is no dependency of the scarcity charges on noise production, and hence no incentive to use newer and less noisy aircraft.

The model also takes the runway capacity limits on competing main airports into account to prevent unrealistic predicted growth on these airports as a result of the limited capacity on the main airport(s) under consideration.

6 Case study 1: Amsterdam airport capacity planning

The AEOLUS model has originally been developed and applied for the Dutch Ministry of Transport, Public Works and Water Management, under supervision of aviation experts from airports, airlines and the national economic research centre. The case study reported here investigated what possible capacity problems might arise for Amsterdam airport (Schiphol) for the years 2020 and 2040, under four different macro-economic and technological scenario assumptions. The welfare effects were evaluated, and a series of 14 different policy measures was investigated to mitigate the adverse societal effects.

The results of this study were used as an input for the scenario policy assessment that the Ministry of Transport, Public Works and Water management together with other ministries completed on the future of Amsterdam Schiphol airport. This assessment was a key input to the new Dutch government policy decision concerning the future of the airport.

The scenario assessment is based on macro-economic scenarios for the Netherlands that were developed by the Netherlands bureau for economic policy analysis [5]. The implications of these four scenarios for air travel through Amsterdam airport are summarized in Figure 6.

Figure 6: Four futures for air travel in 2020.

The two dimensions in Figure 6 represent possible orientations of economic development for Europe and the Netherlands:

- Emphasis on private responsibilities or on public responsibilities?
- Emphasis on international cooperation or national sovereignty?

Figure 7 shows the predicted numbers of flights in 2020 for all four scenarios for each of the three assumptions:

- no runway or noise restrictions, which represents the unconstrained potential demand for air travel on Amsterdam airport;
- the current policy scenario, with existing runway and noise restrictions, and with a slot allocation system based on grandfathering rights;
- an alternative capacity constrained scenario, with a new slot allocation system based on slot trading.

For the two high economic growth scenarios (Global Economy and Transatlantic Markets) the potential demand in 2020 exceeds the existing capacity constraints, in particular the noise limits. The slot trading system is clearly more efficient in that it is able to accommodate more flights within the existing noise capacity constraints. This is mainly due to the fact that this system has noise-generation dependent scarcity charges that stimulate the use of new and more quite aircraft.

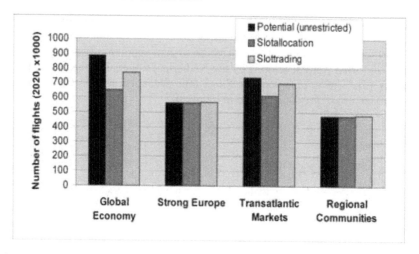

Figure 7: Model forecast of the number of flights per year in 2020 for the four scenarios for three cases (no capacity constraints, slot allocation based on grandfathering rights and slot allocation based on free trading).

Other charging schemes and policies that have been simulated are reported in [6].

7 Case study 2: The impact of air flight tax in the Netherlands

In 2007 Dutch Government decided to levy a tax on air flights to and from all airports in the Netherlands. The objective was to generate 350 million Euro per year. But the exact implementation was still under discussion: it was not yet specified which travellers would pay and which would be exempt from this tax. The Dutch Ministry of Finance commissioned a study to investigate the expected effects, and to decide about the preferred specification of the tax. The AEOLUS model was used for this. In this section, we discuss five of these alternative implementations.

Sixteen alternative versions of the ticket tax have been studied. These versions differed in the amount of tax that each of the segments (departing passengers, transferring passengers, freight) had to pay. In all versions, the total amount of tax collected per year was 350 million Euro. In the remaining of this section, we discuss five of these versions. Since this chapter concentrates on passenger choices, we have only selected versions with no tax on freight (Table 2). The names of the versions correspond to the names in the original report [7].

The AEOLUS model simulates the effects of the ticket tax in 2011 by increasing the fare of air travel starting from the year of introduction of the tax, 2008. Four macro-economic scenarios were simulated, the same as the ones mentioned in the previous section.

Table 2: Effects of ticket tax (introduced in 2008) for the year 2011.

	Version 1	Version 1E	Version 1E-B	Version 2	Version 2E
Tax per departure					
European destinations	€ 23.00	€ 16.67	€ 12.50	€ 13.75	€ 9.50
Intercont. destinations	€ 23.00	€ 37.50	€ 47.50	€ 13.75	€ 21.38
Tax per transfer					
Europe–Europe	–	–	–	€ 13.75	€ 9.50
Europe–ICA	–	–	–	€ 13.75	€ 15.44
ICA–ICA	–	–	–	€ 13.75	€ 21.38
Amsterdam					
Total passengers	−10 to −12%	−8 to −11%	−8 to −10%	−19 to −22%	−20 to −26%
Dep. total	−13 to −14%	−11 to −12%	−10 to −11%	about −10%	about −9%
Dep. Europe	−15 to −16%	about −12%	−9 to −10%	−11 to −12%	about −9%
Dep. interc.	−8 to −9%	−11 to −14%	−14 to −18%	−6 to −7%	−9 to −10%
Transferring	−5 to −8%	−5 to −7%	−4 to −8%	−37 to −39%	−44 to −48%
Total flights	−9 to −12%	−8 to −9%	−8 to −9%	−17 to −20%	−17 to −23%
Regional airports					
Dep. passengers	−18 to −20%	−14 to −16%	−11 to −13%	−13 to −15%	−9 to −12%
Emissions (Amsterdam)					
Noise (dBA)	about −0.3	−0.2 to −0.3	−0.2 to −0.3	−0.7 to −0.8	−0.9 to −1.0
Particles	−5 to −10%	−5 to −9%	−3 to −9%	−14 to −19%	−17 to −23%

For the discussion of the effects of the ticket tax, we distinguish between departing and transferring passengers. Note that a transfer passenger has to pay the tax twice per journey, since he makes a transfer both during the outward trip and the return trip. Arriving passengers do not pay a tax. However, since most passengers buy a round-trip ticket, we assume that half of the tax applies to the outward journey and half of it applies to the return journey. Therefore, the effects on arriving passengers are in the model identical to the effects on departing passengers.

Version 1: Tax on departing passengers only

In this version, each passenger departing from a Dutch airport (except transfer passengers) has to pay a tax of € 23. As a result, less travellers will use a Dutch airport as their departure airport. The number of departing passengers at Schiphol airport decreases by 10–12% in 2011 (depending on the macro-economic scenario, see Table 2). As a result, the number of flights will be reduced. This affects transfer passengers since they have fewer options to travel via Amsterdam. This results in a decrease of transfer passengers of 5–8%.

For European destinations the relative increase in air fare is larger than for intercontinental destinations. Hence, the decrease of the number of travellers that depart from Amsterdam to a European destination is larger than for an intercontinental destination (15–16% vs. 8–9%). Since the regional airports offer mainly European destinations, and they lack the segment of transfer passengers that do not have to pay a tax, regional airports are stronger affected than Amsterdam airport (decrease of total number of passengers of 18–20% for regional airports vs. a decrease of 10–12% for Amsterdam).

Version 1E: Differentiation between European and intercontinental destinations

In this version of the ticket tax departing passengers with a European destination have to pay a tax of € 16.67, while passengers with an intercontinental destination have to pay a tax of € 37.50. As a result, the decrease of the European market at Amsterdam is similar to the decrease of the intercontinental market (about 12%).

Version 1E-B: Further differentiation between European and intercontinental destinations

In this version of the ticket tax departing passengers with a European destination have to pay a tax of € 12.50, while passengers with an intercontinental destination have to pay a tax of € 47.50. As a result, the decrease of the European market at Amsterdam is less than the decrease of the intercontinental market (9–10% vs. 14–18%). Regional airports are less affected than in versions 1 and 1E: the decrease of the total number of passengers for regional airports is about the same as for Amsterdam airport (11–13% for regional airports vs.8–10% for Amsterdam).

Version 2: Tax on departing and transferring passengers

Transfer passengers pay the same amount of tax (per transfer) as departing passengers. In order to raise 350 million Euro per year, the tax level is set at € 13.75. This results in a very strong decrease in the number of transfer passengers (37–39%). This is due to the fact that these passengers have to pay the tax twice per round journey, since they will make a transfer both during the outward and the return trip. Furthermore, these passengers have a large number of good alternatives, because most of them can also choose to make a transfer at London Heathrow, Frankfurt or Paris Charles de Gaulle without paying extra tax or having to make a detour.

Version 2E: Differentiation between European and intercontinental destinations

This version is similar as version 2, but the amount of tax depends on the destination (tax for intercontinental destinations is about 2.25 times as high as for Europeans destinations). This has an even larger effect on transferring passengers (that are predominantly passengers with an intercontinental origin or destination). The decrease of the total number of passengers at Amsterdam airport is 20–26%, while the decrease at regional airports is limited to 9–12%.

Effects of ticket tax on departing passengers

In all versions presented, the number of passengers departing from Dutch airports will decrease. Instead, they will:

- depart from a foreign airport, where they do not have to pay the ticket tax;
- travel using another mode (either train or car). This is only an alternative for travel within Europe;
- decide not to travel at all.

Figure 8 displays the number of passengers (absolute number of passengers, as determined after averaging over the four macro-economic scenarios), who change their travel behaviour for each version of the ticket tax (departure and arriving together). The total number of passengers that no longer depart from/arrive at a Dutch airport (either Amsterdam, or at one of the regional airports) is equal to the number of passengers that either shift their departure/arrival to a foreign airport (about 45%), or shift to a different mode (about 10%) or no longer travel (about 45%).

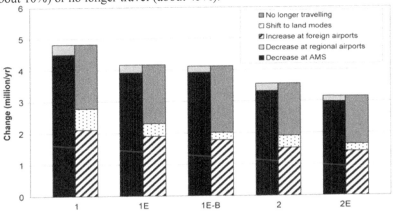

Figure 8: Effect of ticket tax on passengers departing/arriving at Dutch airports (2011).

Effects of ticket tax on transfer passengers

Travellers that stop transferring at Amsterdam airport as a result of the introduction of the ticket tax will instead:

- transfer at another airport;
- shift to a direct flight;
- decide not to travel at all.

Figure 9 displays the effect on the number of transfer passengers at Amsterdam, Frankfurt and Paris Charles de Gaulle. In versions 1, 1E and 1E-B, the number of transfer passengers at Frankfurt and Charles de Gaulle reduces as well. These are travellers that would have departed from a Dutch airport and would have transferred at FRA or CDG if there would not have been a ticket tax. In versions 2 and 2E, the number of transfer passengers at Frankfurt and Charles de Gaulle increases. These are travellers that have diverted their route due to the ticket tax at Amsterdam airport.

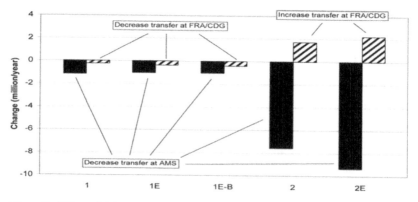

Figure 9: Effect of ticket tax on passengers transferring at Amsterdam airport (2011).

Final implementation

In order to mitigate the effects of the ticket tax on the airlines and airports (particularly on the regional airports), the Dutch government decided to implement a version that is very similar to version 1E-B. It was decided that the tax would be € 11.25 for all destinations within 2500 kilometres, including all EU member countries) and € 45 for other destinations. An exception is made for countries with destinations on both sides of the 2500 kilometres border. The low tax of € 11.25 also applies for other destinations in those countries, provided that they are not further away than 3500 kilometres.

This tax was implemented in the Netherlands on 1 July 2008, and its effects were quickly noticeable. The number of passengers departing from foreign airports increased substantially according to travel agencies. One of these agencies (D-reizen) reported an increase of 350% for their customers [8]. Amsterdam airport announced that their passenger growth would stagnate [9].

KLM expected to loose half a million to a million passengers in 2008 [10]. These effects were reinforced by the impact of the economic crisis that followed in 2008. Early 2009 the Dutch government decided to abandon the tax from 1 July 2009 onwards.

8 Conclusion

In this chapter, we have described a practical demand forecasting model that has been developed for strategic planning purposes. The model has been applied in several studies in the Netherlands, two of which have been described. But, the concept is generic and can easily be applied to simulate demand at airports elsewhere; for instance in other countries, both for main and regional airports. As an example, the model has been successfully implemented in 2007 for forecasting air passenger demand in France, in particular for the various airports in the Paris region.

Having discussed some of the main features and capabilities of the AEOLUS model system, it is also useful at this point to discuss some of its limitations.

1. First we would like to emphasize that the AEOLUS model presented here is a simple, pragmatic forecasting model that uses fairly straightforward methods. It is far from the state-of-the-art methodologies that are described for instance by [11]. That is related to its key objective, and to the requirements of transparency and intuitivity of operation.
2. Another limitation is the fact that the coefficients of several of the models have not been formally calibrated, but were 'imported' from other similar studies. To our defence, we can say that we have, of course, extensively tested the response characteristics of the model, and the resulting demand elasticities. Also our model has been audited by the Netherlands Bureau for Economic Policy Analysis, with favourable outcome. But empirically calibrated coefficients would still add further credibility.
3. Then the supply model, which is a very simple, again highly pragmatic heuristic that has no solid foundation in economic theory. Particularly the way in which the observed multidimensional distribution of aircrafts is modified in response to cost increases would benefit from further work, both in terms of methodology and use of marginal cost functions.
4. The equilibrium procedure: we use a heuristic iterative procedure that adjusts (shadow) costs and passes these on to demand (generalized cost of air passengers) and supply (marginal cost for airlines) until demand and supply are more or less in equilibrium. This problem could be re-specified as a multidimensional optimization problem that could be solved by means of dedicated solvers. In fact we have now implemented a new version of AEOLUS using the General Algebraic Modelling System (GAMS) [12] package.

A final issue that we want to raise is the fact that this type of model is quite demanding in terms of availability of data. Firstly, it requires extensive passenger survey information (including detail about trip origin, destination, journey purpose, air route and socio-economic information) for at least one important airport under consideration, and ideally more. But also it needs detailed airside level of service information, which can be derived from the OAG database [2] and airport statistics. And landside level of service, which can be derived from surface transport networks for road and rail. In return, however, it also provides a mass of information, thus enabling a detailed assessment of future developments and possible impacts of policy measures.

Acknowledgements

The development, implementation and application of the AEOLUS model system has been commissioned by the Dutch Ministry of Transport, Directorate General of Transport and Aviation. Also I want to acknowledge the substantial contributions to the development of the AEOLUS model system that have been provided by Marco Kouwenhoven (Significance) and Jan Veldhuis (SEO).

References

[1] Ben-Akiva, M. & Lerman, S.R., *Discrete Choice Analysis, Theory and Application to Travel Demand*, The MIT Press: Cambridge, MA, 1985.
[2] See www.oag.com.
[3] Kroes, E., Lierens, A. & Kouwenhoven, M., The Airport Network and Catchment area Competition Model ERSA Conference Series, 2005. Available via http://www.ersa.org/ersaconfs/ersa05/papers/521.pdf
[4] Brons, M., Pels, E., Nijkamp, P. & Rietveld, P., *Price Elasticities of Demand for Passenger Air Travel*, Tinbergen Institute Discussion Papers 01-047/3, Tinbergen Institute, 2001.
[5] Mooij, R. de & Tang, P. Four futures of Europe CPB special publication nr. 49. Available via http://www.cpb.nl/nl/pub/cpbreeksen/bijzonder/49/download.html
[6] SEO and RAND Europe, Ontwikkeling Schiphol 2020–2040 bij ongewijzigd beleid – Eindrapport, in opdracht van het ministerie van Verkeer en waterstaat, Directoraat Generaal Transport en luchtvaart (Dutch version only), 2006.
[7] Significance, SEO Economisch Onderzoek, Effecten van verschillende heffingsvarianten op de Nederlandse Luchtvaart, Significance report 07014, 2007 (Dutch version only). Available via http://www. significance.nl/reports/2007-MINFIN-07014.pdf.
[8] NRC, Schiphol verwacht stagnatie door vliegbelasting, news paper article published on 4 January 2008 (Dutch version only). Available via http://www.nrc.nl/economie/article881801.ece/Schiphol_verwacht_stagnati e_door_vliegbelasting
[9] Volkskrant, Duur Schiphol verkeert in crisis, news paper article published on 3 July 2008 (Dutch version only). Available via www.volkskrant.nl/economie/article1039362.ece/Duur_Schiphol_verkeert_in_crisis

[10] Volkskrant, Vliegtaks kost KLM 'miljoen passagiers', newspaper article published on 17 July 2008 (Dutch version only). Available via www.volkskrant.nl/economie/article1043932.ece/Vliegtaks_kost_KLM_miljoen_passagiers.

[11] Hess, S. & Polak, J.W., Mixed logit modelling of airport choice in multi-airport regions. *Journal of Air Transport Management*, **11(2)**, pp. 59–68, 2005.

[12] See www.gams.com.

Regional airports and opportunities for low-cost carriers in Australia

A. Collins, D. A. Hensher & Z. Li
The University of Sydney, Australia

Abstract

Australia is vitally dependent on aviation services for delivering passenger accessibility to many rural and remote locations. The majority of airports in Australia are regional airports. There are real opportunities for a number of regional airports to improve their services for the region through the introduction of low-cost carriers (LCCs). The aim of this paper is to investigate this potential, through a formal model system of the entire aviation network in Australia, focusing on identifying influences on passenger demand and flights offered, and the role of air fares and number of competitors on each route.

Keywords: regional airports; low-cost carriers; regular passenger transport; structural equation system; three stage least squares (3SLS)

1 Introduction

Australia is vitally dependent on aviation services for delivering passenger accessibility to many rural and remote locations. In 2005–06, over 40.93 billion passenger kilometres or 11.47% of the total domestic passenger transport task (including metropolitan travel) was serviced by aviation [1]. Conservatively this represents over 46% of all intra- and inter-state aircraft movements and 13% of revenue passenger activity. As the Australian population progressively, albeit slowly, migrates away from the capital cities along the coast and inland, a number of towns that were once small centres servicing a hinterland have grown to become sizeable hubs for substantial regional activity. The role of aviation has grown in response to the need for improved accessibility to these regional hubs. Some of these centres already enjoy one or more low-cost carriers (LCCs), whereas a number of them are yet to benefit from LCCs, often with a single carrier with relatively high fares and poor service frequency.

There are real opportunities for a number of regional airports to improve their services for the region through the introduction of LCCs. The aim of this paper is to investigate this potential, through a formal model system of the entire aviation network in Australia, focusing on identifying influences on passenger demand and flights offered, and the role of air fares and number of competitors on each route.

The chapter is organized as follows. Section 2 provides an overview of airline activity and regional airports in Australia, with a particular focus on the growth in LCCs, expansion by regional airports and the interplay between the two. Section 3 establishes a formal modelling framework through which operational changes by airlines and airports can be evaluated. Section 4 outlines the data that was collected for model estimation, and provides some summary statistics using this data. Section 5 provides results for the base year for the various models. Section 6 assesses the impact of new LCC entrants on patronage and regional airport activity. The chapter concludes with a summary of major findings.

2 An overview of airline activity and regional airports in Australia

2.1 Airline activity

Prior to 1990, the Australian domestic aviation market was a regulated duopoly on the trunk routes. The two permitted airlines, Ansett Airlines and Australian Airlines, were similar in their operation and engaged in little competition. Entry by other airlines was prohibited, capacity constraints were applied by the government, and fares were determined on a cost-plus basis. The first hint of liberalization came in 1981 with an amendment of the Airlines Agreement Act that allowed regional airlines to expand their operations on non-trunk routes and operate jet aircraft. On 1 November 1990 the entire industry was deregulated. Restrictions on capacity, fares and entry were lifted, opening the way for new airlines to enter the market and compete.

Compass Airlines was the first new entrant to the market, commencing flights just 1 month after economic deregulation. Compass intended to compete as a low-cost carrier and undercut the bloated costs of the incumbent airlines. Its fleet comprised of a single aircraft type, the 266 seat A300–600. The network was simple, linking only seven major airports. Interestingly, this approach contrasts with later entrants, who have relied on smaller Boeing 737 and A320 aircraft, and formed networks that extend well beyond the major airports (although admittedly while being significantly more capitalized). Despite having lower costs than the incumbent airlines, Compass Airlines collapsed barely a year after commencing operations. Nyathi et al. [2] provide an extensive analysis of why Compass failed, and consider the implications of undercapitalization, poor pricing including crude discounting strategies, the lack of a yield management system, poor marketing and management and a lack of access to adequate terminal space. The Compass brand was revived in 1992 as Compass Mk II when a new startup called Southern Cross Airlines decided to trade under the same name. It too failed, and no LCCs operated for the remainder of the decade.

Despite the absence of further LCC entrants, Australian domestic aviation did not remain static in the decade that followed deregulation. In August 1992, Australian Airlines was purchased by Qantas. Qantas in turn was privatized by the Australian government in March 1993. Forsyth [3] determined that Qantas and Ansett increased their total factor productivity during the 1990s, but not to the levels of equivalent overseas airlines. Hence, there was scope for new entrants to compete at a lower cost. Ansett however struggled in the more competitive environment. A lack of capital under the full ownership of Air New Zealand, few changes to labour arrangements, maintenance problems, high costs and the entrance of Virgin Blue in August 2000 all placed pressure on the airline (Forsyth [4]). Ansett went into administration in September 2001 and ceased operation in March 2002.

Virgin Blue, the first successful Australian LCC, was a major beneficiary of the Ansett collapse. The sudden decline in domestic seat capacity allowed Virgin Blue to expand rapidly with a competitive low-cost model. Old Ansett terminal space was also easily acquired at most airports. A lack of adequate terminal space had played a key role in the demise of Compass Airlines. The case against Qantas claiming anti-competitive behaviour disadvantaging Compass in respect of adequate information at Sydney Airport on the location of the Compass gates, was won by Compass but only after the airline had ceased operations. Virgin Blue commenced operations in August 2000 between Brisbane and Sydney. By April 2003, it was operating 24 aircraft and moving 6.6 million passengers per year. By the end of 2007, Virgin Blue was operating 53 aircraft and moving 15.3 million passengers per year. In May 2007 Virgin Blue had a domestic market share of 31.7%, making it the second largest domestic airline in Australia. Virgin Blue has also proven very profitable, with a profit every year since its formation, and a 2007 profit of A$215.8 million.

While Virgin Blue is recognized as a LCC, some signs suggest that it lies somewhere between the LCC and full-service models. The airline has introduced various services that LCCs have typically eschewed. Airport lounges were opened in April 2003 and a frequent flier programme commenced in November 2005. A two class configuration was introduced in March 2008, with a premium economy fare providing extra seat pitch and the use of the middle seat as a table. These new features suggest that Virgin Blue is attempting to both cater to the leisure market and compete with Qantas in the high yield business market.

Virgin Blue has expanded beyond the trunk routes linking the capital cities, and beyond the traditional tourist routes linking the capitals with the larger coastal tourist destinations such as Cairns and Townsville (see Figure 1). Recent route additions have previously been served only by regional airlines, including Sydney-Albury and Sydney-Port Macquarie. To make these thin routes viable, Virgin Blue is in the process of supplementing its core Boeing 737 fleet with 24 Embraer 170 and 190 regional jets, which carry 76 and 104 passengers, respectively. The Albury destination was selected from a short list of 20 regional airports, which were considered with the Embraer jets in mind [5]. The size of both the Embraer acquisition and the short list suggest that further expansion to regional airports can be expected, and boosts the relevance of the analysis in this chapter. In a further indication of the airline's desire to grow business patronage, one of the stated aims of the Embraer acquisition is to boost frequency on key business routes [6], while presumably retaining load factors (LFs) and profitability.

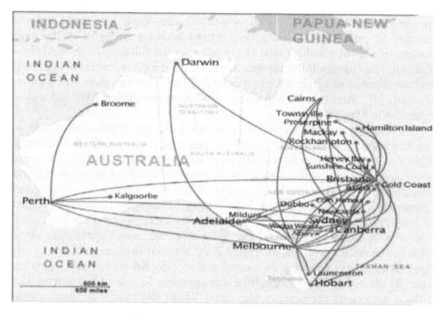

Figure 1: Network structure for the top 46 city pairs in Australia (ITLS mapping 2008).

Qantas was not prepared to let the entry of a LCC go unchecked, and in response re-branded Impulse Airlines as Jetstar and commenced operations in May 2004. Impulse had originally been an independent regional airline, but in 2000 commenced operations as a LCC using Boeing 717s. The airline encountered cash flow problems, and by April 2001 Impulse was wet leasing its aircraft to Qantas. In November 2001 Impulse was acquired by Qantas. Wholly owned by Qantas, Jetstar is an LCC that operates independently and is run by a different management team. Unlike Virgin Blue, Jetstar does not attempt to lure business travellers; they are served by Qantas. Jetstar does not have airport lounges or multiple classes on domestic routes. Qantas' frequent flier points can be earned on the more expensive fares, but Jetstar does not run its own programme.

In the 2006/2007 financial year, Jetstar carried 7.6 million passengers with 24 A320s, and held 15% of the domestic market share. The average cost per available seat kilometre (CASK) is a common measure used to identify how low cost an airline is. Jetstar had the lowest CASK of all Australian airlines, at 7.5 cents in 2007. By comparison, Virgin Blue, the other LCC, had a CASK of 8.2

cents in 2007. Compared with LCCs, traditional carriers, particularly regional airlines, have much higher CASKs. For example, the CASK was 22.1 cents for Regional Express (REX) and 19.7 cents for Skywest. The Qantas Group (including Qantas, QantasLink and Jetstar) had a CASK of 11.5 cents in 2007. This figure would be higher if Jetstar was excluded from the calculation (figures sourced from various annual reports).

In 2007, Jetstar was awarded the title of 'World's Best Low-Cost Airline', based on a survey run by Skytrax Research [7]. Air Berlin and EasyJet were awarded second and third place, respectively. This survey also listed Virgin Blue as the second best LCC in the Australia/Pacific region.

Tiger Airways Australia is an LCC that commenced operations in November 2007. The airline is a part of the Tiger Aviation group, which also includes Tiger Airways Singapore. Initial routes have centred on Melbourne Tullamarine airport as a hub, with 13 destinations served by five A320s as of April 2008. Sydney and Brisbane are notable for their absence in the list of initial destinations, with the nearest served destinations to each being Newcastle and the Gold Coast, respectively. Tiger Airways' chief executive has suggested that these major airports have not been serviced as they do not offer sufficiently low costs or the required level of efficiency [8]. By contrast, Tullamarine was able to offer Tiger a low-cost terminal. This is evidence that LCCs are actively considering airport charges as they choose destinations, and a motivation for the inclusion of airport charges in our models.

The full-service and LCCs are complemented by a variety of regional airlines, which in recent years have undergone a degree of consolidation. QantasLink is operated by Qantas and is comprised of three regional airlines: Airlink, Eastern Australia Airlines and Sunstate Airlines. Regional Express, also known as Rex, was formed as a merger of Hazelton Airlines and Kendell Airlines, two profitable airlines that were owned by Ansett at the time of its collapse. Skywest operates regional routes primarily in Western Australia, as well as charter operations that cater to the booming mining industry in that state.

The Australian domestic aviation market is now highly competitive, with one full-service carrier and three LCCs. Competition has been fierce on existing routes, but the LCCs are also seeking to expand by introducing new routes and destinations that have previously only been served by regional airlines. There is growing evidence of the potential of Australia's regional airports to grow passenger traffic with additional LCC's. The model developed below addresses this issue.

2.2 Regional airports

Only Sydney, Melbourne, Brisbane, Perth and Adelaide have over five million passengers per annum. Using this number of passengers per annum as the threshold for the definition of a regional airport, all remaining airports can be defined as regional. There is a great variability in the regional airports with regards to the mix of inbound and outbound passenger flows. Some are significant population centres and trip generators in their own right. Other regional airports largely serve inbound tourist flows, including many of the airports along the Queensland coast.

In the late 1990s, many Australian airports were privatized. For example, Townsville airport is now owned by Queensland Airports Limited, a regional airport investment company. Privatization has allowed for a capital injection into many airports, and has led to a greater focus on passenger growth and airport profit. Other regional airports are owned by the surrounding local council(s), either directly, as with Albury and Port Macquarie airports, or indirectly through a company, as with Newcastle airport. Here the motivation is typically to support and grow tourism and business in the local area.

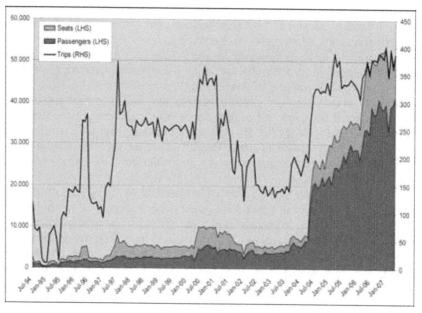

Figure 2: Monthly revenue passenger movements, seats and aircraft trips for Newcastle–
Brisbane route.

Newcastle airport is a good case study example of a regional airport that has been a beneficiary of LCC operations. Figure 2 details revenue passenger movements, seat capacity and aircraft trips between Newcastle and Brisbane from July 1994 to May 2007. From 1997 to 1999, when the route was serviced by regional airlines, the route is notable for its high frequency of service, steady passenger flows and low LF (an average of 48.8%). In May 2000, Impulse Airlines commenced operations on the route with Boeing 717s, resulting in modest increases in passenger flow but little change in LF. At that time, the airline was moving from a regional to a low-cost model. However, by November 2001, Impulse was integrated into QantasLink, Qantas' regional operator. Seat capacity and passenger flows receded to pre-2000 levels. The boost in passenger movements created by Impulse Airlines' presence was small compared to the almost immediate quadrupling of passenger movements to 20,000 per month following the entry of both Virgin Blue and Jetstar on the route in May 2004. As of mid-2007, passenger movements had doubled again to an average of 40,000 per month. The number of monthly aircraft trips following the entry of the LCCs was not unprecedented, however the use of larger aircraft lead to substantially greater seat capacity.

The substantial increase in passenger movements at Newcastle airport is likely to have numerous causes. In addition to increased capacity and reduced fare price resulting from the entry of Virgin Blue and Jetstar, the nature of Newcastle as a trip origin and destination must be considered. Located 20 kilometres north of Newcastle (and 150 kilometres north of Sydney), Newcastle airport primarily serves the Hunter region, which has a population of 573,000. Additionally the Central Coast, a sizeable and growing population region, has the potential to be a part of the catchment area. For many Central Coast residents, a road journey to Newcastle airport would involve a similar distance, similar or shorter travel time and less expensive parking than Sydney airport. Therefore, the airport has an extensive outbound market. The Hunter region also boasts numerous tourist attractions, including wineries and coastal holiday destinations. The combination of increased service by LCCs, reduced fares and a strong potential for trip production through a populous catchment area makes Newcastle airport a great example of the growth that regional airports and LCCs can experience by working in tandem.

Given the background on airline and airport activity in Australia, and the growing role of LCCs, the rest of the paper focuses on the development and application of a model system to represent the key demand and supply elements of aviation activity, with a specific interest in identifying the opportunities to grow passenger activity at specific airports through the introduction of LCCs.

3   Establishing a framework in which to investigate the role of regional airports and airline activity

The previous section described both the growth in LCC operations in Australia, and the impact this increase has had on some Australian regional airports. In this section, we establish a formal framework through which we can analyse the underlying drivers supporting the development of a regional airport or entry of a new operator such as a low-cost airline.

The development of a demand model to predict base regular passenger transport (RPT) flows on each route between points A and B in a network begins with a theoretical definition of the potential influences on RPT flows. The literature on factors influencing airline travel by a specific carrier is extensive (see for example [9], Chapter 3). The major influences can be synthesized under the broad headings of fare, service levels, the nature of the end points (i.e. productions and attractions), presence of competitors and the capacity of an airline to serve a market. Using a framework proposed by Dresner and Windle [10], formally we can specify a demand function as in equation (1) as follows:

$$PASS_{j,AB} = f\{FARE_{j,AB}, COMP_{j,AB}, SERVICE_{j,AB}, MARKET_{j,A}, MARKET_{j,B}\}. \quad (1)$$

PASS is the annual passengers carried by airline j between points A and B including both origin and destination passengers and flow-through passengers. FARE is a vector of fares offered by airline j between points A and B. These fares are not the full fare paid by a flow-through passenger, and would mainly influence the origin–destination passengers. COMP acknowledges the role of competitors on the route that affects both total demand and airline share. COMP could be generalized to include competition from other modes such as the car, train or coach. In the current study we confine the demand context to the airline market. We can distinguish between LCCs and other carriers. SERVICE is a vector of service (quality) attributes such as headways between flights, on-board service, type of aircraft and airline image/reputation. MARKET refers to the characteristics at the production and attractions ends of the AB endpoints. Total population and its wealth as measured by per capita and household income are often used as indicators of production and attraction.

A closer assessment of equation (1) will suggest that some of the explanatory variables are endogenous. For example, air fare can be considered endogenous because changes in passenger levels may trigger changes in prices, especially in a liberalized competitive market. Endogenous fares are themselves a function of a number of potential influences as summarized in equation (2).

$$FARE_{j,AB} = f\{PASS_{j,AB}, SERVICE_{j,AB}, MARKET_{j,A}, MARKET_{j,B}, COMP_{j,AB}, LF_{j,AB}, DIST_{AB}\}. \quad (2)$$

The additional attributes on the right hand side are stage length distance (DIST) of a route, which is a useful proxy for the cost of flying that route, and LF which gives some idea of flight productivity and hence is linked to cost to the airline of servicing each passenger. We also postulate that the number of competitors on a route is also endogenous, dependent on the size of the market as shown in equation (3).

$$COMP_{j,AB} = f\{MARKET_{j,A}, MARKET_{j,B}\}. \quad (3)$$

Finally, the number of flights between each city pair is endogenous to the extent that it is influenced by patronage on the demand side and competition on the supply side. It is potentially influenced by airport landing and passenger charges.

$$FLIGHTS_{j,AB} = f\{PASS_{j,AB}, COMP_{j,AB}, AIRPORTCHG_{j,AB}\}. \quad (4)$$

As no airline-specific passenger and fare data are available, j is neglected for this study. Thus, instead of airline specific data, city-pair data is used for modelling such as the passenger number for all airlines serving on a pair and the average fare for all operating airlines. We have taken the natural logarithm of each continuous variable as one possible functional specification for assessment. This enables us to obtain mean estimates of direct elasticities from the parameter estimate of the explanatory variable.

The structural equation system of four interdependent equations is a set of simultaneous equations. We have chosen three stage least squares (3SLS) to obtain parameter estimates, which starts with either two stage least squares (2SLS) or seemingly unrelated regression (SUR). The rationale is set out below. 2SLS is a single equation method, which means that over identifying restrictions in other equations are not taken into account in estimating parameters in a particular equation. As a result, 2SLS estimates are not asymptotically efficient. The system method of 3SLS uses information concerning the endogenous variables in the system and takes into account error covariances across equations, and hence is asymptotically efficient in the absence of specification error. The SUR method uses information about contemporaneous correlation among error terms across equations in an attempt to improve the efficiency of parameter estimates.

The 2SLS method uses instrumental variable methods which involve substituting a predicted variable for the endogenous variable Y when it appears as a regressor. Hence the predicted variables are linear functions of the instrumental variables and the endogenous variable substitutes $\hat{Y}$ or Y, which results in consistent estimates. Normally, the exogenous variables of the system are used as the instruments. It is possible to use variables other than exogenous variables from the system of equations as instruments; however, the estimation may not be as efficient. For consistent estimates, the instruments must be uncorrelated with the residual and correlated with the endogenous variable.

SUR may improve the efficiency of parameter estimates when there is contemporaneous correlation of errors across equations. In practice, the contemporaneous correlation matrix is estimated using ordinary least squares (OLS) residuals. Under two sets of circumstances, SUR parameter estimates are the same as those produced by OLS: when there is no contemporaneous correlation of errors across equations (the estimate of contemporaneous correlation matrix is diagonal); and when the independent variables are the same across equations.

Theoretically, SUR parameter estimates will always be at least as efficient as OLS in large samples, provided that the equations are correctly specified. However, in small samples the need to estimate the covariance matrix from the OLS residuals increases the sampling variability of the SUR estimates, and this effect can cause SUR to be less efficient than OLS. If the sample size is small and the across-equation correlations are small, then OLS should be preferred to SUR. The consequences of specification error are also more serious with SUR than with OLS.

The 3SLS method combines the ideas of the 2SLS and SUR methods. Like 2SLS, the 3SLS method uses $\hat{Y}$ instead of Y for endogenous regressors which results in consistent estimates. Like SUR, the 3SLS method takes the cross-equation error correlations into account to improve large sample efficiency. For 3SLS, the 2SLS residuals are used to estimate the cross-equation error covariance matrix. 3SLS is at least as efficient as any other estimator which uses the same amount of information.

4 Model data

4.1 Sourcing of data for model estimation

The publicly available data reported by The Federal Bureau of Infrastructure, Transport and Regional Economics (BITRE) aggregates revenue passenger movements for each city pair, such that we are unable to identify passengers carried by each operator between a pair of end points. Further, data is not available for routes with only one operator. No reasonable basis was found for either of these two restrictions; the airlines claim the airline-specific information is commercially sensitive. Thus, instead of airline-specific passenger data, city pairs at the airport level are considered in this paper to identify the mutual relationships between passenger numbers, fares and competition.

Traffic data for domestic and regional airline activity in Australia for the top 46 city pairs served by multiple airlines in the financial year 2006/2007 was provided by BITRE [11]. All data at the city pair level is an aggregation of both directions. That is, the city pair of Albury–Sydney aggregates the traffic information both from Albury to Sydney and from Sydney to Albury. All city pair figures are for direct flights between the two cities. For example, a flight from Melbourne to Brisbane via Sydney will count both for the Melbourne–Sydney pair and the Sydney–Brisbane pair. The data provides scheduled RPT information including revenue passenger movements, aircraft movements, available seats, LFs, revenue passenger kilometres (RPKs) and available seat kilometres (ASKs). The 46 city pairs cover over 84.8% of total domestic passenger movements and around 60.8% of total domestic aircraft trips for Australia in 2007.

For each city pair, the number of traditional and LCCs was obtained from the Airline On-time Performance Annual Report for the 2007 financial year [12], which indicated the competition on each city pair. This report also has airline-specific trip data (e.g. sectors flown, cancellations, departures/arrivals on time, departures/arrivals delayed) for different routes; thus the proportion of each airline with respect to frequency in those city pairs can be calculated and the competition on routes can be revealed. However, airline-specific passenger numbers have not been found at the city pair level and requests for such data from each airline were singularly unsuccessful. Monthly lowest fare information on the top 70 city pairs were provided by BITRE, in four categories where available. The categories are business, full economy (transferable and fully refundable), restricted economy (transferable and non-refundable) and best discount (cheapest fare). The lowest restricted economy fares were averaged into annual figures for modelling. In addition to traffic related information, distances in kilometres between airports for 46 city pairs were obtained from BITRE [13].

The characteristics of an airport and its surrounding region are crucial. Providing low charges may help airports attract LCCs. Landing charges and passenger charges are two main categories for RPT services. Landing charges (or runway charges) are based on per tonne of maximum take-off or landing weight (MTOW). Passenger charges are levied per arriving/departing passenger through the domestic terminal including a terminal usage charge and an aeronautical passenger charge. For freight services, a freight (or cargo) charge is calculated on per tonne of goods discharged from or loaded into aircraft. While many Australian airlines typically transport freight in addition to passengers, freight charges have not been included in the models. Airport charging rates were obtained by directly contacting individual airports or local councils. All charges and fares include a goods and services tax (GST) of 10%. Annual inbound and outbound passenger movements from all destinations were obtained for each airport from BITRE [14]. All airports are identified by International Air Transport Association (IATA) codes.

Information describing the area surrounding the airport was gathered, including (1) population and weekly per capita income at the local area or district where an airport is located [15], and (2) accommodation statistics (i.e. the total number of beds in hotels, motels and serviced apartments with five or more rooms) at the tourism regional level [16].

Table 1 provides a summary of all city pair level data available for model estimation.

Table 1: Data available for model estimation.

Variable	Description
PopulatA	Local area population at Airport A
PopulatB	Local area population at Airport B
IincomeA	Median individual weekly income for the local area where Airport A is located
IincomeB	Median individual weekly income for the local area where Airport B is located
HincomeA	Median household weekly income for the local area where Airport A is located
HincomeB	Median household weekly income for the local area where Airport B is located
NobedsA	Number of beds in the tourism region where Airport A is located
NobedsB	Number of beds in the tourism region where Airport B is located
PaxA	Annual total passengers at Airport A
PaxB	Annual total passengers at Airport B
LandCA	Landing charge for Airport A
LandCB	Landing charge for Airport B
PaxCA	Passenger charge for Airport A
PaxCB	Passenger charge for Airport B
Distance	Distance between airports (kilometers)
AvFare	Average restricted economy fare for a city pair in the 2007 financial year
Pax	Annual total passenger movement number for a city pair
Seat	Annual total seat number for a city pair
RPK	Annual total Revenue passenger kilometers (000s)
LF	Load factor
ASK	Annual total available seat kilometers (000s)
Nocomp	Number of competitors for a city pair (traditional and LCCs)
NoLCA	Number of LCCs for a city pair
Alltrip	Annual total aircraft trip number for a city pair

4.2 Overview of available data

The approach to model estimation is strictly cross-sectional. Thus, the predicted passenger flows are essentially the long-run profile under a specified network configuration. When developing an appropriate data set for model estimation, we must ensure that we have a sufficiently large sample that has a rich variability in the set of variables that we wish to test as possible sources of influence on passenger flows. We have a total of 46 city pair observations, serviced by six airlines (two LCCs, three regional carriers and one traditional carrier). Table 2 lists the airlines that serve each of the 46 city pairs. Tiger Airways began operations in November 2007, and so is not included in the data.

Table 2: Routes under study.

Port A	Code A	Port B	Code B	Airlines operating on route
Albury	ABX	Sydney	SYD	QantasLink and Regional Express
Adelaide	ADL	Brisbane	BNE	Jetstar*, Virgin Blue* and Qantas
Adelaide	ADL	Canberra	CBR	Virgin Blue* and Qantas
Adelaide	ADL	Melbourne	MEL	Virgin Blue* and Qantas
Adelaide	ADL	Gold Coast	OOL	Jetstar* and Virgin Blue*
Adelaide	ADL	Perth	PER	Virgin Blue* and Qantas
Adelaide	ADL	Sydney	SYD	Jetstar*, Virgin Blue* and Qantas
Broome	BME	Perth	PER	Virgin Blue*, Qantas, QantasLink and Skywest
Brisbane	BNE	Canberra	CBR	Virgin Blue*, Qantas and QantasLink
Brisbane	BNE	Cairns	CNS	Jetstar*, Virgin Blue* and Qantas
Brisbane	BNE	Darwin	DRW	Jetstar*, Virgin Blue* and Qantas
Brisbane	BNE	Hobart	HBA	Jetstar* and Virgin Blue*
Brisbane	BNE	Hamilton Island	HTI	Jetstar* and Virgin Blue*
Brisbane	BNE	Melbourne	MEL	Jetstar*, Virgin Blue* and Qantas
Brisbane	BNE	Mackay	MKY	Jetstar*, Virgin Blue* and QantasLink
Brisbane	BNE	Newcastle	NTL	Jetstar*, Virgin Blue* and QantasLink
Brisbane	BNE	Perth	PER	Virgin Blue* and Qantas
Brisbane	BNE	Proserpine	PPP	Jetstar* and Virgin Blue*
Brisbane	BNE	Rockhampton	ROK	Jetstar*, Virgin Blue* and QantasLink
Brisbane	BNE	Sydney	SYD	Virgin Blue* and QantasLink
Brisbane	BNE	Townsville	TSV	Jetstar*, Virgin Blue* and Qantas

Table 2: Routes under study (continued).

Port A	Code A	Port B	Code B	Airlines operating on route
Ballina	BNK	Sydney	SYD	Jetstar*, Virgin Blue* and Regional Express
Canberra	CBR	Melbourne	MEL	Virgin Blue*, Qantas and QantasLink
Canberra	CBR	Sydney	SYD	Virgin Blue*, Qantas and QantasLink
Coffs Harbour	CFS	Sydney	SYD	Virgin Blue* and QantasLink
Cairns	CNS	Melbourne	MEL	Jetstar*, Virgin Blue* and Qantas
Cairns	CNS	Sydney	SYD	Jetstar*, Virgin Blue* and Qantas
Dubbo	DBO	Sydney	SYD	QantasLink and Regional Express
Darwin	DRW	Melbourne	MEL	Jetstar* and Virgin Blue*
Hobart	HBA	Melbourne	MEL	Jetstar*, Virgin Blue* and Qantas
Hobart	HBA	Sydney	SYD	Jetstar*, Virgin Blue* and Qantas
Hervey Bay	HVB	Sydney	SYD	Jetstar* and Virgin Blue*
Kalgoorlie	KGI	Perth	PER	Qantas and QantasLink
Launceston	LST	Melbourne	MEL	Jetstar*, Virgin Blue*, Qantas and QantasLink
Launceston	LST	Sydney	SYD	Jetstar* and Virgin Blue*
Sunshine Coast	MCY	Melbourne	MEL	Jetstar* and Virgin Blue*
Sunshine Coast	MCY	Sydney	SYD	Jetstar* and Virgin Blue*
Melbourne	MEL	Mildura	MQL	QantasLink and Regional Express
Melbourne	MEL	Newcastle	NTL	Jetstar*, Virgin Blue* and QantasLink
Melbourne	MEL	Gold Coast	OOL	Jetstar* and Virgin Blue*
Melbourne	MEL	Perth	PER	Jetstar*, Virgin Blue* and Qantas
Melbourne	MEL	Sydney	SYD	Jetstar*, Virgin Blue* and Qantas
Gold Coast	OOL	Sydney	SYD	Jetstar*, Virgin Blue* and Qantas
Perth	PER	Sydney	SYD	Virgin Blue* and Qantas
Sydney	SYD	Townsville	TSV	Jetstar*, Virgin Blue* and Qantas
Sydney	SYD	Wagga Wagga	WGA	QantasLink and Regional Express

Note: *Denotes a LCC.

The network structure for those 46 city pairs is visualized in Figure 1. State capitals are in a larger font. A large percentage of cities are located on the Eastern seaboard, which is reflective of Australia's geographic population distribution.

Revenue passenger movements for all city pairs in the financial year 2006/2007 are given in Figure 3, with movements varying from a high of 6,624,665 for Melbourne–Sydney to a low of 121,056 for Darwin–Melbourne. The top three pairs link Sydney, Melbourne and Brisbane, and together account for approximately 40% of all revenue passenger movements. Of the top 46 pairs, 36 have less than 1,000,000 annual passenger trips. Gold Coast–Sydney is the fourth largest pair by revenue passenger movements, and the largest that includes a regional airport (Gold Coast). Figure 4 indicates the annual number of aircraft trips for each city pair, with flights varying from 41,907 for Melbourne–Sydney to 835 for Darwin–Melbourne.

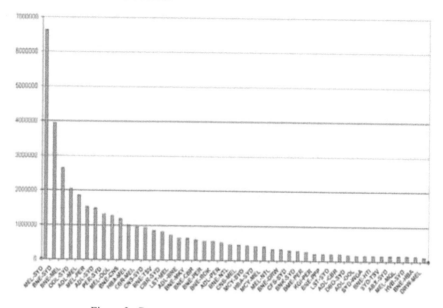

Figure 3: Revenue passenger movements for city pairs.

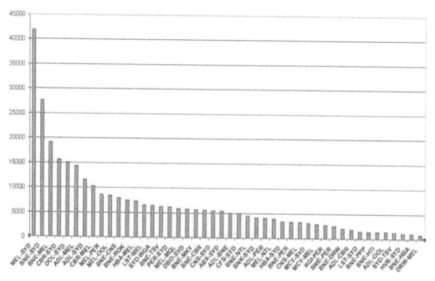

Figure 4: Total aircraft trips for city pairs.

The LF indicates the proportion of total aircraft seats that are filled by revenue passengers [17], which is a key parameter to establish seat utilization over routes. Figure 5 presents LFs for the top 46 city pairs in Australia. The average LF is 0.78; Melbourne–Gold Coast has the highest LF (0.87), while the LF for Sydney–Wagga Wagga is the lowest (0.66). The majority (76.1%) of pairs generate LFs between 0.75 and 0.80, which reveals efficient utilization on those top pairs in general.

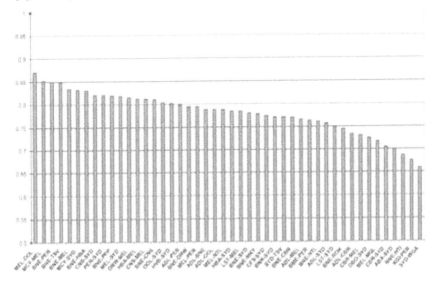

Figure 5: Load factors for city pairs.

Average lowest air fares and distances between airports are shown in Figure 6. Distances range from 236 kilometres to 3615 kilometres, while fares range from A$199.00 to A$598.70. Generally, there is consistency in price for any given distance, with fares increasing with distance. However, some routes have notably higher costs per kilometre than other routes of similar distance. Examples include Albury–Sydney, Kalgoorlie–Perth and Sydney–Wagga Wagga, all of which have no low-cost airline. The absence of LCC competition might be contributing to the high fares. However, high costs per kilometre for Broome–Perth, which is serviced by the LCC Virgin Blue, suggests that other factors are also at play.

A total of 27 airports are in the domestic and regional network under study. Table 3 shows the airports served by each of the airlines in the study.

From Table 3, only Sydney, Melbourne, Brisbane, Perth and Adelaide have over five million passengers per annum. Using this number of passengers per annum as the threshold for the definition of a regional airport, all remaining airports can be defined as regional. Thus, 10 of 46 routes link primary airports, while the remaining 36 routes link a primary airport with a regional airport. Given that the total number of passengers for all of Australia's airports was 112,068,399 for the financial year 2006/2007 [14], the 27 airports analysed cover 94.9% of total airport passenger movements.

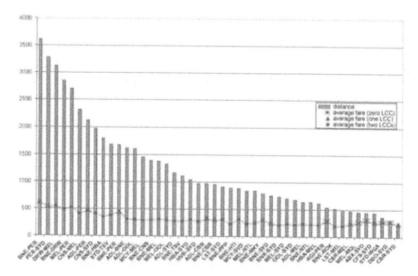

Figure 6: Average fares and distances between airports.

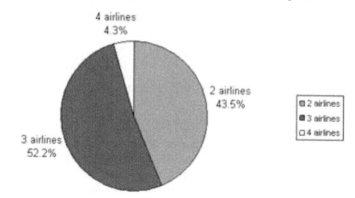

Figure 7: Profile of competition on routes.

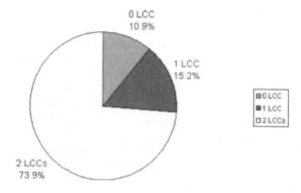

Figure 8: Profile of competition on routes by low-cost airline.

Of the 46 city pairs involved in this study, which are all served by more than one airline, the majority (52.2%) of them are served by three airlines (see Figure 7). With respect to LCCs, Virgin Blue and Jetstar compete with each other on 34 pairs or 73.9% of total city pairs, and only 10.9% of them are not served by any LCC (see Figure 8). These figures reveal the high level of competition on the top routes in Australia.

Table 3: Ports served by airlines in the study.

Airport	Passengers	Airlines					
		A	B	C	D	E	F
Sydney	31,016,186	✓	✓	✓	✓	✓	
Melbourne	22,156,871	✓	✓	✓	✓	✓	
Brisbane	17,379,809	✓	✓	✓	✓		
Perth	7,977,091	✓	✓	✓	✓		✓
Adelaide	6,181,390	✓	✓	✓			
Cairns	3,782,183	✓	✓	✓			
Gold Coast	3,777,856	✓	✓	✓			
Canberra	2,687,336		✓	✓	✓		
Hobart	1,629,417	✓	✓	✓			
Darwin	1,403,685	✓	✓	✓			
Townsville	1,271,649	✓	✓	✓			
Launceston	995,664	✓	✓	✓	✓		
Newcastle	958,087	✓	✓		✓		
Sunshine Coast	880,822	✓	✓				
Mackay	743,321	✓	✓		✓		
Rockhampton	638,602	✓	✓		✓		
Hamilton Island	465,941	✓	✓				
Broome	344,790			✓	✓		✓
Ballina	323,791	✓				✓	
Coffs Harbour	323,565				✓		
Proserpine	256,282	✓			✓	✓	
Albury	212,264				✓	✓	
Kalgoorlie	211,857			✓	✓		
Wagga Wagga	203,798				✓	✓	
Hervey Bay	189,429	✓	✓				
Dubbo	171,026				✓	✓	
Mildura	167,983				✓	✓	
Total number of airports served	*10,635,0695*	*19*	*22*	*14*	*17*	*8*	*2*

Note: For airlines, where: A=Jetstar; B=Virgin Blue; C=Qantas; D=QantasLink; E=Regional Express; F=Skywest.

5   Results of base year models

The passenger demand model, the air fare model, the competition model and the flight supply model are estimated simultaneously, addressing feedback between the left-hand side variables. The final passenger demand model for the financial year 2007 is presented in Table 4. A number of alternative functional forms were investigated in the process leading to the selection of the preferred model. All the explanatory variables have the expected sign and are statistically significant at the 5% level of significance. The measure of overall goodness-of-fit (R^2) must be treated with caution in simultaneous equations. For two-stage least squares, some of the regressors enter the model as instruments when the parameters are estimated. However, since our objective is to estimate the structural model, the actual values, not the instruments for the endogenous right-hand-side variables, are used to determine the model sum of squares (MSS). The model's residuals are computed over a set of regressors. We have been able to explain 44.3% of the single-equation variation in passenger numbers between the 46 pairs by the differences in five right hand variables and a constant.

What we find is that the number of passengers travelling between each location pair is inversely related to average fare and directly related to population at origin and destination, the number of competitor airlines on the route and the presence of one or more low-cost airlines (1,0).

As a double logarithmic form, the parameter estimates can be directly interpreted as elasticities. For example, −1.18778 indicates that a 1% increase in average fare, *all other things being equal*, results in a 1.18778% reduction in the demand for passenger movements per annum. The key drivers of passenger demand are total population at two end points of a pair and the competition on a route. The presence of LCCs is also expected to stimulate more passengers. There are two main reasons for this. First, capacity for that route increases with more airlines in service, and secondly the air fare decreases due to increasing competition, particularly from a low-cost airline. This is also supported by the air fare model given in Table 5. All right-hand side variables are statistically significant at the 5% level of significance, except the presence of LCCs which is significant at the 10% level. 38.8% of the variation in fares can be explained by the five influences. The average fare varies inversely with the number of passengers (the quantity effect) and the presence of one or more LCCs; and directly by the median personal income at the origin and destination as well as the LF.

Table 4: Preferred passenger demand model.

Right hand side variables	Acronym	Final full model (*t*-ratio in brackets)
Ln (average fare)	LNAVFARE	−1.18778 (−2.84)
Ln (the number of competitors)	LNCOMP	1.54455 (2.46)
Ln (product of populations at the local area for airports A and B)	LPOPAB	0.21791 (3.96)
Dummy variables (1,0) for the presence of one more LCCs	LCC	0.72730 (2.07)
Constant		12.0174 (4.54)
R^2		0.443
Adjusted R^2		0.388
No. of observations		46

Note: Dependent variable: Natural logarithm of the number of passenger movements.

Table 5: Preferred air fare model.

Right hand side variables	Acronym	Final full model (*t*-ratio in brackets)
Ln (the number of passengers)	LNPAX	−0.0939 (−2.54)
Ln (product of weekly per capita income at the local area for Airports A and B)	LNPINCAB	0.8256 (3.13)
Ln (load factor)	LNLF	2.71243 (3.62)
Dummy variables (1,0) for the presence of one or more LCCs	LCC	−0.25676 (−1.87)
Constant		−2.4103 (−0.75)
R^2		0.388
Adjusted R^2		0.328
No. of observations		46

Note: Dependent variable: Natural logarithm of the average fare.

Table 6 summarizes the findings for the competition model. All right hand side variables except the constant are statistically significant at the 5% level of significance. The number of airlines competing on the route is positively related to the presence of one or more low-cost airlines (1,0) and the median weekly household income at the origin and destination.

Finally, as summarized in Table 7, the number of flights between a pair of airports is positively influenced by patronage demand. As passenger demand grows, airlines respond by adding more capacity on the route. The implied mean elasticity of 0.7842 indicates that a 10% increase in passengers, all other factors held constant, lead to an average 7.84% increase in flights. Importantly, the number of flights is inversely related to the product of landing and passenger charges at each airport in the pair, supporting the position that airport charges do have a statistically significant influence on attracting air services. This could be more significant to low-cost airlines, as they are more cost-sensitive than traditional carriers.

Table 6: Preferred competitor airlines model.

Right hand side variables	Acronym	Final full model (*t*-ratio in brackets)
Ln (product of median weekly household income at the local area for airports A and B)	LNHINC AB	0.34978 (1.96)
Dummy variables (1,0) for the presence of one or two LCCs	LCC	0.30362 (3.17)
Constant		−4.2007 (−1.64)
R^2		0.208
Adjusted R^2		0.148
No. of observations		46

Note: Dependent variable: Natural logarithm of competitor number on each route.

Table 7: Preferred air trip supply model.

Right-hand-side variables	Acronym	Final full model (*t*-ratio in brackets)
Ln (the number of passengers)	LNPAX	0.78421 (–2.16)
Ln (the product of landing and passenger charges at each airport in the pair)	LNAPCHAB	–0.00046 (–2.13)
Constant		–1.8719 (–2.11)
R^2		0.758
Adjusted R^2		0.747
No. of observations		46

Note: Dependent variable: Natural logarithm of the number of flights between a pair.

6 Scenario assessment – introduction of low-cost carriers (LCCs)

The model system developed in the previous section can be used to undertake scenario analysis. In particular, we are interested in what would be the impact of key policy instruments such as fares, new entrants on a route, especially LCCs on patronage and hence on regional airport activity; and also what influence does airport charges and patronage growth have on the amount of flight activity to and from a regional airport.

We have set up a scenario model to evaluate a range of 'what if' applications. A reduced form of the four structural equations is used in scenario applications. The reduced-form models of interest are the natural log of passenger movements between each airport pair and the natural log of the number of flights between airport pairs.

The patronage prediction model is:

$$Ln(Pax) - [(-1.18778) \times (-0.09389) \times Ln(Pax)] = 12.0174$$
$$-1.18778 \times [-2.41027 + 1.187786 \times Ln(pincAB)] + 2.71243 \times Ln(LF) - 0.25676 \times LCC]$$
$$+1.54455 \times [-4.20066 + 0.34978 \times Ln(hincAB) + 0.30362 \times LCC]$$
$$+0.21791 \times Ln(popAB) + 0.72730 \times LCC,$$

$$Ln(No. \text{ of Flights}) = -1.87193 - 0.00046 \times Ln(landchg \times passchj) + 0.78421 \times Ln(Pax).$$

The patronage model can be simplified by rearranging terms to result in:

$$Ln(Pax) = \{8.391 - 0.98057 \times Ln(pincAB) - 3.22177 \times Ln(LF) + 1.50122 \times LCC$$
$$+ 0.540253 \times Ln(hincAB) + 0.21791 \times Ln(popAB)\} / 0.888479.$$

These models have been calibrated (via the constant) to produce the relationship shown in Table 8 between actual patronage and predicted patronage on each airport pair. Table 9 is the relationship between actual and predicted flights per annum. The discrepancy is less than 1000 passenger trips per annum.

Table 8: Calibrated airport pairs patronage.

Airport pair	Actual pass	Pred pass	Diff pred vs. act
ABX–SYD	155,609	154,935	–674
ADL–BNE	643,579	644,297	718
ADL-CBR	201,511	201,215	–296
ADL–MEL	1,862,257	1,862,220	–37
ADL–OOL	173,876	174,414	538
ADL–PER	533,226	533,895	669
ADL–SYD	1,483,330	1,483,515	186
BME–PER	268,445	268,106	–339
BNE–CBR	595,824	596,154	331
BNE–CNS	1,191,234	1,191,173	–61
BNE–DRW	330,579	330,168	–411
BNE–HBA	137,256	137,081	–175
BNE–HTI	164,358	164,129	–228
BNE–MEL	2,632,646	2,632,322	–324
BNE–MKY	626,685	627,126	441
BNE–NTL	463,982	464,348	366
BNE–PER	563,713	563,532	–181
BNE–PPP	202,663	203,035	372
BNE–ROK	563,093	563,532	439
BNE–SYD	3,934,916	3,935,407	492
BNE–TSV	851,283	851,746	463
BNK–SYD	284,532	285,227	695
CBR–MEL	954,650	955,363	714
CBR–SYD	829,103	829,047	–57
CFS–SYD	300,740	301,060	320
CNS–MEL	458,447	458,119	–328
CNS–SYD	946,381	945,735	–646
DBO–SYD	181,099	181,173	74
DRW–MEL	121,055	120,846	–209
HBA–MEL	1,001,491	1,001,610	119
HBA–SYD	426,258	426,279	21
HVB–SYD	150,317	149,828	–489
KGI–PER	211,145	211,855	710
LST–MEL	725,924	725,122	–802
LST–SYD	202,016	202,806	791
MCY–MEL	410,118	409,813	–305
MCY–SYD	444,053	444,406	353

Table 8: Calibrated airport pairs patronage (continued).

Airport pair	Actual pass	Pred pass	Diff pred vs. act
MEL–MQL	152,711	153,373	663
MEL–NTL	339,083	338,827	–256
MEL–OOL	1,273,399	1,272,959	–440
MEL–PER	1,539,857	1,539,652	–205
MEL–SYD	6,624,596	6,624,613	17
OOL–SYD	2,051,743	2,051,485	–257
PER–SYD	1,321,133	1,320,831	–302
SYD–TSV	158,816	159,575	760
SYD–WGA	167,745	168,392	647
Average	844,706	844,790	84

Table 9: Calibrated airport pairs flights.

Airport pair	Actual flights	Pred flights	Diff Pred vs. Act
ABX–SYD	5390	4855	–535
ADL–BNE	4992	5492	500
ADL–CBR	1853	2209	356
ADL–MEL	14,334	14,828	494
ADL–OOL	1357	1968	611
ADL–PER	4050	4739	689
ADL–SYD	11,610	11,683	73
BME–PER	2504	2766	262
BNE–CBR	5614	5169	–445
BNE–CNS	7950	8900	950
BNE–DRW	2085	2536	451
BNE–HBA	1058	1635	577
BNE–HTI	M	1883	–
BNE–MEL	19,157	19,845	689
BNE–MKY	5713	5378	–335
BNE–NTL	4536	4249	–287
BNE–PER	3257	3667	410
BNE–PPP	1449	2219	770
BNE–ROK	7493	8154	661
BNE–SYD	27,648	28,025	378
BNE–TSV	6292	7189	897
BNK–SYD	M	2896	–
CBR–MEL	10,308	9605	–703

Table 9: Calibrated airport pairs flights (continued).

Airport pair	Actual flights	Pred flights	Diff Pred vs. Act
CBR–SYD	15,587	14,905	–682
CFS–SYD	M	3024	–
CNS–MEL	3235	3733	498
CNS–SYD	5520	6395	876
DBO–SYD	5818	5253	–564
DRW–MEL	835	1481	646
HBA–MEL	7331	7769	437
HBA–SYD	3351	3976	625
HVB–SYD	1144	1756	612
KGI–PER	2700	2291	–409
LST–MEL	6572	6036	–536
LST–SYD	1539	2214	675
MCY–MEL	2880	3490	610
MCY–SYD	3081	3752	671
MEL–MQL	M	5235	–
MEL–NTL	3976	3323	–653
MEL–OOL	8436	8658	222
MEL–PER	8577	9369	792
MEL–SYD	41,907	41,747	–159
OOL–SYD	15,081	15,067	–14
PER–SYD	6159	6802	643
SYD–TSV	1283	1833	550
SYD–WGA	6453	6043	–410
Average	6880	7044	164

Note: M = missing in data.

If we increase the number of LCCs on routes where there is currently no low-cost carrier, five in total, at flight levels typically provided on other regional routes, then we observe a substantial increase in potential patronage as summarized in Table 10 (i), and the prediction of additional flights (Table 10 (ii)) to accommodate the extra demand and existing LFs. Selecting the Albury–Sydney pair as an example, there is the potential to grow 180,815 passenger trips in both directions per annum with 11 LCC flights daily. This amounts on average to 5.5 flights in each direction per day for an extra 247 passengers in each direction per day, a payload per flight of close to 45 passengers. This seems a sensible set of estimates to attract a LCC.

We investigated the influence of airport charges on the number of flights offered to establish if it was having a significant influence on flights offered out of specific airports. Table 11 shows that the sensitivity to airport landing and passenger charges is very small indeed, consistent with the elasticity parameter in Table 6. Hence on our evidence we can discount this as a major determinant of airline choice of activity to regional airports.

Table 10: Impact of introducing an LCC on routes without LCCs

(i) Patronage impact.

Airport pair (two-way)	Pred pass	Base pred pass	Diff
ABX–SYD	335,750	154,935	180,815
DBO–SYD	392,609	181,173	211,436
KGI–PER	459,097	211,855	247,242
MEL–MQL	332,366	153,373	178,993
SYD–WGA	364,911	168,392	196,520

(ii) Number of new flights required.

Airport pair	New pred flights	Base pred flights	Diff pred vs. actual	Extra one-way flights daily	Extra pass/day	Pass per extra flight
ABX–SYD	8803	4816	3987	11	495	45
DBO–SYD	9563	5213	4350	12	579	49
KGI–PER	4183	2275	1908	5	677	130
MEL–MQL	15,337	8335	7003	19	490	26
SYD–WGA	11,028	5995	5033	14	538	39

Table 11: Impact of 10% reduction in airport charges at key regional airports.

City Pair	Flights pred	Flights actual	Increase
BNE–MKY	5226	5219	6
BNE–NTL	9288	9277	11
BNE–PPP	2404	2402	3
BNE–ROK	7600	7590	9
BNE–TSV	6320	6313	8
MEL–NTL	9680	9668	12
SYD–TSV	5509	5503	7
SYD–WGA	2150	2148	3

7 Conclusions

This paper has reviewed the progress of aviation activity and development of services to and from regional airports in Australia, as background to the development of a model system capable of identifying the factors influencing the demand for passenger movements and number of flights between airport pairs in Australia. The modelling framework also recognized the endogeneity of air fares and the number of competitors in the determination of the market for regional aviation activity.

For regional airports that currently are not serviced by LCCs, five in total, we investigated the opportunities to grow patronage and increase flights in the context of ensuring an acceptable payload per flight. The opportunity gap in the market is shown to exist. This is encouraging and indeed we are aware that a LCC is planning to service Albury in 2008.

Acknowledgements

Jonathan Firth of the Bureau of Infrastructure, Transport and Regional Economics (BITRE) provided extensive support in sourcing published and unpublished data, as did Theo Koo of the University of New South Wales. Thanks also to Larry Dwyer and Peter Forsyth for advice.

References

[1]   Department of Infrastructure, Transport, Regional Development and Local Government, *Australian Transport Statistics Yearbook 2007*, Canberra: Australian Government, 2008.

[2]   Nyathi, M., Hooper, P. & Hensher, D.A., Compass Airlines: 1 December 1990 to 20 December 1991: What went wrong? Parts I and II. *Transport Reviews*, **13**, pp. 119–149, 185–206, 1993.

[3]   Forsyth, P., Total factor productivity in Australian domestic aviation. *Transport Policy*, **8**, pp. 201–207, 2001.

[4]   Forsyth, P., Low-cost carriers in Australia: Experiences and impacts. *Journal of Air Transport Management*, **9**, pp. 277–284, 2003.

[5]   Virgin Blue, Ho Ho Ho – It's off to Albury we go! http://www.virginblue. com.au/AboutUs/Media/NewsandPressReleases/P_002088.htm on 3 April 2008.

[6]   Virgin Blue, Virgin Blue Orders 20 Embraer 'E-Jets' – New Fleet Strategy for Australia's 'New World Carrier', http://www.virginblue.com.au/ AboutUs/Media/NewsandPressReleases/U_001189.htm.

[7]   Skytrax Research, World Airline Awards, http://www.worldairlineawards. com/Awards_2007/Lowcost.htm.

[8]   The Australian, Tiger vows to shun high-cost airports, http://www. theaustralian.news.com.au/story/0,25197,22687139-23349,00.html.

[9]   Trethaway, M.W. & Oum, T.H., *Airline Economics: Foundations for Strategy and Policy*, Centre for Transportation Studies, University of British Columbia: Vancouver, 1992.

[10] Dresner, M. & Windle, R., Are US air carriers to be feared: Implication of hubbing to North Atlantic competition. *Transport Policy*, **2(3)**, pp. 195–202, 1995.

[11] BITRE, Domestic Airline Activity, http://www.btre.gov.au/info.aspx? NodeId=101.

[12] BITRE, Airline on Time Performance Annual Reports, http://www. bitre.gov.au/publications/17/Files/Master200607.xls.

[13] BITRE, Australian Air Distances, http://www.btre.gov.au/Info.aspx?NodeId=97.

[14] BITRE, Airport Traffic Data, http://www.btre.gov.au/Info.aspx?NodeId=96.

[15] Census, Census of Population and Housing, http://www.abs.gov.au/websitedbs/d3310114.nsf/Home/census.

[16] ABS, Tourist Accommodation, Small Area Data, http://www.abs.gov.au/AUSSTATS/abs@.nsf/DetailsPage/8635.3.55.001Jun%202007?OpenDocument.

[17] BITRE, Avline, http://www.btre.gov.au/Info.aspx?ResourceId=606&NodeId=92.

Subject Index

WITPRESS   ...for scientists by scientists

Railway Timetabling, Operations Analysis and Rescheduling

Edited by: I. HANSEN, Delft University of Technology, The Netherlands

The book comprises a number of research papers presented at several Computers in Railways Conferences. It has been compiled by Ingo A. Hansen, President of the International Association of Railway Operations Research (IAROR) and comprises selected papers originating from different countries, such as Denmark, France, Germany, Japan, Italy, Netherlands, Sweden and Switzerland. The papers give an overview of the current state-of-the-art analytical approaches, methods and simulation tools for the modelling and analysis of network timetables, the distribution of train delays and real-time rescheduling of perturbed operations. The topics include e.g. railway capacity estimation according to the UIC norm 406, train punctuality analysis based on standard track occupation and clearance data, and boarding, alighting and distribution of passengers along suburban trains, as well as fast recognition and resolution of conflicts between train movements in case of disturbances by means of real-time speed adaptation, re-ordering or re-routing. The book can serve as an introduction to the theory of railway traffic, timetable design, operations analysis, simulation, safety and control for Master and PhD students from engineering faculties and professionals working in the railway industry.

ISBN: 978-1-84564-500-7   eISBN: 978-1-84564-501-4
Forthcoming   apx 208pp   apx £79.00

WITPRESS *...for scientists by scientists*

Urban Transport XVI

Urban Transport and the Environment in the 21st Century

Edited by: **A. PRATELLI**, *University of Pisa, Italy and* **C.A. BREBBIA**, *Wessex Institute of Technology, UK*

This International Conference on Urban Transport and the Environment has been successfully reconvened annually for the last fifteen years. Transportation in cities, with related environmental and social concerns, is a topic of the utmost importance for urban authorities and central governments around the world. Urban Transport systems require considerable studies to safeguard their operational use, maintenance and safety. They produce significant environmental impacts and can enhance or degrade the quality of life in urban centres. The emphasis is to seek transportation systems that minimize any ecological and environmental impact, are sustainable and help to improve the socio-economic fabric of the city. Another area of concern addressed by the conference is that of public safety and security, seeking ways to protect passengers while retaining the efficiency of the systems.

The sixteenth conference topics are: Transport Modelling and Simulation; Transport Security and Safety; Transport Technology; Land Use and Transport Integration; Intelligent Transport Systems; Public Transport Systems; Road Pricing; Inter-Model Transport Systems; Transport Automation; Traffic Management; Urban Transport Strategies; Urban Transport Management; Environmental Impact, Including Air Pollution and Noise; Information Techniques and Communications; Mobility Behaviour; Policy Frameworks; Environmentally Friendly Vehicles; Transport Sustainability; Safety of Users in Road Evacuation.

WIT Transactions on The Built Environment, Vol 111
ISBN: 978-1-84564-456-7   eISBN: 978-1-84564-457-4
Forthcoming   apx 700pp   apx £266.00

Power Supply and Energy Management

Edited by: **E. PILO**, *Pontifical Comillas University of Madrid, Spain*

In latter years, energy efficiency has become a crucial concern for every transportation mode, but it is in electrified railways where energy savings have shown a bigger potential due to (i) regenerative braking, that allows converting kinetic energy into electric power, and (ii) vehicle interconnection, that allows other trains to use regenerated power. Power supply and energy management will continue to develop in the future.

This book gathers under a single cover several papers published in the Computer on Railways series (IX, X and XI) and focuses on power supply and energy management. Some of the discussed themes are: modelling, simulation and optimisation of AC and DC infrastructure, analysis of rolling stock consumption, and innovative approaches in power supply operation.

This book will be invaluable to management consultants, engineers, planners, designers, manufacturers, operators and IT specialists who need to keep abreast of the latest developments in the field.

ISBN: 978-1-84564-498-7   eISBN: 978-1-84564-499-4
Forthcoming   apx 192pp   apx £73.00

WIT eLibrary

WITPRESS   ...for scientists by scientists

Computers in Railways XII

Computer System Design and Operation in the Railway and Other Transit Systems

Edited by: **B. NING**, *Beijing Jiaotong University, China and* **C.A. BREBBIA**, *Wessex, Institute of Technology, UK*

This volume features the proceedings of the Twelfth International Conference on Computer System Design and Operation in the Railway and other Transit Systems. This book updates the use of computer-based techniques, promoting their general awareness throughout the business management, design, manufacture and operation of railways and other advanced passenger, freight and transit systems. It will be of interest to railway managers, consultants, railway engineers (including signal and control engineers), designers of advanced train control systems and computer specialists.

The COMPRAIL series has become the world forum for all major advances in this important field, and this latest conference volume highlights themes of great current interest. These are: Planning; Safety and Security; Advanced Train Control; Drivers Operations; Communications; Energy Supply and Management; Operations Quality; Timetable Planning; Level Crossing and Obstacle Detection; Computer Techniques; Dynamics and Wheel/Rail Interface; Maintenance; Rolling Stocks; Training Tools and Technology; Condition Monitoring; Asset Management; Maglev and High Speed Railway; Passenger Information Systems; Train Regulations; Metro and Other Transit Systems; Advanced Train Control.

WIT Transactions on The Built Environment, Vol 114
ISBN: 978-1-84564-468-0   **eISBN: 978-1-84564-469-7**
Forthcoming   apx 1000pp   apx £380.00

WIT*Press*
Ashurst Lodge, Ashurst, Southampton,
SO40 7AA, UK.
Tel: 44 (0) 238 029 3223
Fax: 44 (0) 238 029 2853
E-Mail: witpress@witpress.com

CPSIA information can be obtained at www.ICGtesting.com
Printed in the USA
BVOW08*1735230614

356990BV00004B/27/P